THE DOORS OF
LEARNING

BRYANT L. CURETON

THE DOORS OF LEARNING

REFLECTIONS FROM A PRESIDENCY

Elmhurst College

THE DOORS OF LEARNING
published by
ELMHURST COLLEGE

ISBN–13: 978-0-9715120-3-0

Printed in the United States of America

Elmhurst College, 190 Prospect Avenue
Elmhurst, Illinois 60126-3296

Rolland Natural paper stock contains 30% post consumer waste fibers.

Acknowledgements and Dedication

I am deeply grateful to all those who organized the many events that inspired these remarks, to those who prepared this collection with care and professionalism, and to my wife Jeanette, my wisest collaborator, sharpest editor, and closest friend. Ultimately, all these talks are about the students of Elmhurst College—past, present, and future, and it is to them that this book is dedicated.

Table of Contents

Table of Contents

(continued)

Introduction

T alk is the heart of higher education. Other things are essential, like reading and writing; but talk is the strong, spirited center of college life. Not idle talk or crazy talk—those you can find anywhere. The best college talk is purposeful, original, and always searching: for goals, essences, and connections.

This book presents college talk of an exceptional order. It begins with the inaugural address of Bryant L. Cureton, the twelfth president of Elmhurst College, delivered on November 5, 1994, in Hammerschmidt Memorial Chapel on the campus. It ends with comments from the same podium at a Founders Day Convocation nearly fourteen years later, in the final months of Dr. Cureton's transforming presidency of the College. Along the way—at New Student Convocations, Midyear Commencements, and the myriad other special events that season and shape each academic year—President Cureton had occasion to publicly reflect on things that matter: learning and connecting, knowledge and practice, silence and simplicity, the person and the community. This volume represents a partial record of his reflections.

"First and foremost I see myself as a teacher," Dr. Cureton said not long after his arrival at Elmhurst. Here are twenty-nine examples of a master teacher's lessons from an important presidency, which brought sustained growth in the College's curriculum, impact, and prestige. Elmhurst College is proud to present this addition to the record of the Cureton presidency—an era that looks more and more like a turning point in the institution's history.

Foreword

ELMHURST COLLEGE: A VENUE
FOR GRACE AND TRUTH

WALTER BRUEGGEMANN
ELMHURST COLLEGE
CLASS OF 1955

When I matriculated as a freshman at Elmhurst College in the fall of 1951, I found the work assignments to be demanding and intimidating. I studied *Moby Dick* in English 101 with Tekla Storey and understood very little. I cut open a pig's eye in Biology 101 with George Langeler and saw very little. I studied sociology under Th. W. Mueller ("Dean Miller" he was called) who was my most important college teacher, and learned his starchy, uncompromising social criticism that set me on my way. The work was demanding and intimidating and I was a slow starter. Eventually I got the hang of it, and came to see that Elmhurst College was indeed, for all its demand, a venue for grace and truth. We learned, via the white whale, that evil is an obsession that will bring us to defeat. We learned from the pig that the bodily reality of the world is complex and freighted with vitality. We learned from Th. W. Mueller about "pecuniary emulation" and "conspicuous consumption." We were taught the truth about natural reality and social reality, and not to flinch from hard social criticism. But it also became clear, without any imposed religious conviction, that the undergirding of lived reality is permeated with the beauty of holiness and that transformed possibilities await even the power of evil, even the power of rapacious politics, and that even a pig without an eye may come to a "new creation."

This deep subset of "grace and truth" has characterized the College in powerful ways in the Cureton years. And I am delighted to verbalize my thanks to President Cureton for his discerning and courageous leadership in helping to recover much of that rich legacy of the College through his persistent leadership. Along with the visible betterment of the campus and the stabilizing of the financial position of the College, Cureton has never forgotten that the business of the College is education in the classic sense of "liberal." I wrote to the president after he published his column tracing the concept of "mentoring" back to its old Greek narrative context. He has understood that the College, in a variety of ways, is a mentoring enterprise, mentoring and forming students into the legacy of grace and truth. It is emblematic of that deeply rooted legacy that under Cureton the College has placed a statute of Reinhold Niebuhr at the center of the campus. That most famous of our alumni voiced and embodied the truth of the College; and there he stands now, with penetrating eyes, summoning coming generations to embrace that legacy.

Niebuhr was deeply rooted in the founding church tradition of the College, but he held the church tradition loosely enough that none ever had to fear authoritarian imposition from him. But he understood the theological function of truthfulness that is rooted in the God of all truth. The liberal arts tradition that is entrusted to the College is a long-term enterprise of truth-telling amid all of the distortions—ancient and contemporary—of false-telling, propaganda and ideology. The slow, steady power of truth that defies "truthiness" is a practice Cureton has vigorously appropriated. Niebuhr understood as well the theological function of gracefulness which contends that at the bottom of all reality is a gracious spirit that moves underneath and beyond all our efforts at control, a generosity ordained in reality that gives the lie to violence, selfishness, and exclusion. The atmosphere of humaneness that characterizes the College and that extends to the business and science programs reminds us that our common patterns of domination and denial are penultimate and cannot be sustained.

President Cureton retires at something of an ominous moment in our society, when violence abounds, when our social infrastructure weakens, and we seem to have lost our way. The College is left, at his retirement, in a strong position with clarified goals and purposes. Thus I anticipate that in the next coming presidency of the College, Elmhurst will continue to play a large role in education of the human spirit that is quite incommensurate with its resources. I anticipate that the College will continue to be a gathering point for truthfulness, unflinching in its critique of contemporary forms of tribalism and chauvinism and ideological self-deception. I anticipate that the College will continue to be a gathering point for graciousness, insistent in its recognition that the divine mystery of goodness surrounds us and permits us to continue to ponder the wonder of human destiny, even in the face of flawed social practice. I anticipate that the College will have new leadership that will strengthen the College in its distinctive mandate of a humane society and a sustainable environment.

Of course the theme of "grace and truth" is, in Christian tradition, a characterization of Jesus of Nazareth. The wonder of that phrasing in the tradition of Elmhurst is that the claim is generative and not authoritarian, open to new possibility and not a demanding imposition. When I was in Professor Mueller's class on "The Sociology of Race" in 1954, we were in class on the day when word came of the Court ruling on *Brown v. Board of Education of Topeka*. When he heard the news, Mueller—who had worked on race issues for a very long time—broke out in an uncharacteristic jig in front of the class. He never said a word about "grace and truth," but he knew about the truth of compassionate justice and he knew about the grace of attending to the other. Out of that wide knowing about grace and truth that has always marked the College, I have no doubt that it will continue in such passionate, generative ways. The College remains under the surveillance of the sharp eyes of Niebuhr, eyes that have seen clearly and loved dearly and followed nearly. What could be better!

COLUMBIA THEOLOGICAL SEMINARY
DECATUR, GEORGIA
JANUARY 28, 2008

Prepared for delivery at a service in Hammerschmidt Memorial Chapel, May 18, 2008.

1 *Beginnings*

ONE

Designing the Doors of Learning

INAUGURAL ADDRESS
NOVEMBER 5, 1994

O n the surface, ceremonies reflect reality rather than create it. Celebrating a birthday does not make one a year older. And yet, the symbolism of the Circle of Investiture we have just experienced makes a powerful point. If the image of the presidential medallion and chain of office being passed among those who represent us all—bringing us together; linking past achievement, present challenge, and future opportunity; focusing the work of all our hands on our common enterprise—if this image illuminates and clarifies the path that lies before us, then we will today have contributed to the shaping of our community of learners by the way we have celebrated it.

In any case, it is probably therapeutic, from time to time, for an academic community to see its president in chains. To speak for the first time attached in this way to Elmhurst College is an intense experience. What *you* have to worry about for the next few minutes is just what Albert Camus meant when he wrote that "intelligence in chains loses in lucidity what it gains in intensity."

I want to use this brief time before you—and what lucidity I can muster—to reflect on the fundamental purpose of the enterprise that brings us together as communities of learners, and then to focus on one special aspect of the particular academic community at Elmhurst College. I begin by reaching back to a simple act each of us performed this morning, with little or no thought, at the beginning of this ceremony: To enter this room, we walked through a doorway.

Education is the door through which we move into new understanding and new opportunities. It is a way through the wall of ignorance and incompetence that separates us from the fuller exercise of our God-given abilities. The primary business of those of us who labor in the halls of academe is to design the doors of learning. This is not always immediately apparent, as we wrestle with all the secondary tasks of finding and spending money, housing and feeding students, attending endless committee meetings, and explaining ourselves to everyone from prospective students to concerned alumni. But it is when we are planning curricula, choosing what is important to teach, developing syllabi, teaching classes, creating and supporting learning opportunities outside the classroom—it is when we are directly engaged with students in the learning process—that we are designing and building the doors of learning. We cannot go through those doors *for* our students, but we can design them with integrity and creativity and hold them open with encouragement and inspiration.

Come with me on a quick visit to some doors designed far away and long ago, doors that speak to us in a special way today. They are found in a small city in northern France, and they take us back to the middle of the twelfth century. In the west façade of the cathedral at Chartres is a set of three doors surrounded by a profusion of sculpture in a composition that has been known through the centuries as the Royal Portal. These doorways constitute more than an important display of early Gothic art. They also present an eloquent statement of a particular view of life.

The central images on the tympana over these doors represent the religious symbols we would expect, ranging from

4

the birth of Jesus to the Final Judgment. But within the archivolts surrounding the figures of Christ and Mary are three sets of figures that send a striking message over the intervening 850 years. Least surprising, surely, are the figures over the center door—surrounding Christ Triumphant are the twelve apostles and the twenty-four elders of the Apocalypse playing ancient instruments to His glory. The first visitors to the cathedral would have understood clearly this vision of the end of time and its lesson of the centrality of faith.

But when we move to the right-hand door, we find a series of distinctly nonbiblical figures—seven women and seven men. On closer examination, it emerges that each of the women represents one of the liberal arts, as defined by medieval scholars: the Trivium of grammar, logic, and rhetoric, and the Quadrivium of arithmetic, music, geometry, and astronomy. Each figure is shown practicing her special art. Grammar is teaching two unruly little boys, Geometry traces figures on a tablet, Music is playing a set of tuned bells and holds a harp and viol. And beneath each is the figure of a man representing a historic thinker or author, an exponent of that art. Cicero stands with Rhetoric, Euclid with Geometry, Aristotle with Logic, and Pythagoras sits under Music working with pen and blotter at his lap desk.

The timeworn serenity of the stone carvings might lead one to miss the drama of this particular doorway. The burghers of twelfth-century Chartres would probably never have seen the symbols of secular learning raised to these heights and used to frame the figure of Christ himself. And the addition of the pagan authors would have radically compounded the impact of the statement. It is not likely this was an accident or an artistic whim.

In all probability, it was intended as a pointed statement. In the years when the west façade was being built, the city of Chartres was known not for its architecture but for its school.

The leading scholar and chancellor of the Cathedral School was Bishop Thierry, a zealous proponent of the still-controversial notion that human wisdom was compatible with, and indeed might complement, divine wisdom—a notion not well received by significant sectors of the church hierarchy of the time. Thierry had devoted considerable energy to the advocacy of a definition of the educated person that included attention to the skills of reason, and his masterpiece, a sort of handbook of the seven liberal arts, was completed just as the Royal Portal was being planned. We can only guess at the arguments that must have taken place over the idea of including this visual statement of general education requirements in the most visible part of the new cathedral. But in the end there it was—a proud pronouncement that could not be missed by anyone aware of the issues.

Finally, there is the third door to the left. Here we find, surrounding the figure of Christ, another series of secular figures with profound meaning for those who would enter the cathedral. The twelve signs of the zodiac range across the archivolt in fantastic imagery, and under each is a very human figure shown doing the work of that season: April tends fruit trees, July harvests wheat, November slaughters a pig. All those who shared the common cycles of laborers could identify with these images and feel welcome entering beneath them.

What is presented in this remarkable assembly of the Royal Portal is a vision of learning, work, and faith, each expressed with vigor, but linked together in a coherent whole. All three doors lead into the incredible space of the cathedral, and the message they convey of the value and connectedness of these three parts of life's path could not have escaped the pilgrims who journeyed to Chartres. Here was a fresh and daring assertion of wholeness. What it must have meant to walk through those doors!

And what can we say of *our* doors? If we think of the design of the contemporary college experience as a set of doorways into a fuller life of service and continued growth, could an outsider looking at that portal see where our commitments lie and by what lights we teach?

I would argue that one reason for us to be concerned about this question is that higher education has not dealt particularly well with the linkages among the separate elements symbolized by the three doors of the Royal Portal that celebrate liberal learning, meaningful work, and faith. In so many ways, our age of specialization has taken us in a quite different direction. We have disaggregated the pieces of life, and even when we purposely set out to find the common ground, our tendency is to put more of our energy into defending the boundaries than overcoming them.

Days like today, when we celebrate our life together, help us to rekindle our sense of being a college in the pure sense of the word—a *collegium*, a group of colleagues joined in a common pursuit. But there is an even deeper and more powerful reason to seek ways to resist the pull of differentiation even as we respect its contribution: the students we serve are whole people. Our fundamental commitment to our students as whole people is embedded in the soul of colleges like Elmhurst. And so, when we hear Alfred North Whitehead's stern dictum, "You may not divide the seamless coat of learning," we recognize more than a theoretical abstraction. That "seamless coat" serves and warms a person we care about deeply, and we are simply not prepared to send one of our graduates off wearing a pretty good sleeve here, part of an excellent collar there, and maybe a few buttons in the bargain. Our deep commitment sets for us a high standard.

Finding ways to weave together the parts of education we have allowed to fall apart is a major challenge for our entire educational community today. Many of the most intractable problems in academe are in fact only special cases of this general pattern. Science remains outside the intellectual experience of far too many otherwise educated people. In spite of lip service to diversity, we fail to prepare graduates to be leaders in overcoming human differences, arguably *the* fundamental issue of our era. And even at church-related institutions, we fail to recognize the chasm in much of education today between what goes on in the specialized classroom and the struggles of students as they wrestle with—or, worse, do *not* wrestle with—the great questions of life's meaning and purpose.

Each of these important issues deserves our attention, and will, I am confident, continue to find a significant place in our debates and in our efforts at institutional renewal over the coming months and years. But I want to focus for a moment on one great tension in higher education that we at Elmhurst College are in a particularly good position to address. One of the most striking things about this college is the way the two traditions of liberal arts education and preparation for professional careers are linked in a friendly and mutually supportive partnership. And yet we have barely begun to realize the full potential of the synergy of these great traditions in the experience of our students.

It is quite remarkable how diligent American higher education has been in keeping these two pathways apart. We have defined "quality" in liberal arts colleges as the relative absence of programs linked to professional opportunities. And, on the other side, schools and programs with clear occupational objectives have claimed the fast track to "real" success. In some career areas, such as medicine and law, the *modus vivendi* has been the strict separation of general undergraduate from specialized graduate-level work in the professional school. In general, those who see their job as preparing students for meaningful work and those who aim at preparing students to live a rich life have kept each other at arm's length. One is reminded of the years when science was being introduced into the college program and schools such as Harvard and Yale took pains to house the new departments in buildings some distance from the main quadrangle so as not to compromise the real heart of the institution.

Underlying this great separation is a fundamental misreading of both traditions. The notion of liberal learning in fact emerged out of efforts to provide what can only be understood today as professional preparation. If one follows the phrase "liberal arts" back in time—back before *septum artes liberales*, the seven medieval liberal arts; back before the Roman *artes liberales,* the learning appropriate to the freeman—one comes eventually to the earliest formulation, the fifth-century B.C. Greek phrase *enkuklios paideia*—most often translated as "general education."

But interestingly, the phrase is rooted in the word *kuklos*, referring to everyday circles, but probably drawn from the circles of the dancing chorus. In early Greek society, music and the cycles of civic life seemed inextricably intertwined, and the purpose of preparation in the arts was to learn the ways of the community, to become part of the chorus, a performer in the daily struggles and conflicts of the *polis*, and thus fully prepared for civic leadership—the true profession of the citizen. For the Roman student of the liberal arts, a major goal was to become, in Quintilian's words, "the perfect orator, capable of addressing any topic and assuming any position of leadership in the State." The scholars of the Middle Ages did not formulate the seven arts simply as speculative philosophy but as the appropriate pathway to the learned professions. And later, reflecting the same professional purpose of liberal studies, we find Martin Luther lamenting, "Where are the preachers, jurists and physicians to come from, if grammar and other rhetorical arts are not taught?"

If we have in more recent centuries allowed the tradition of liberal learning to be viewed as the opposite of preparing for a career, it is because we have lost our grasp of what the concept meant to the builders of the tradition. Much the same case can be made that the best of professional preparation has always emphasized broadening experiences that reach beyond just the special practical skills of a job. Through the centuries, various forms of apprenticeship or junior status have often been aimed precisely at providing a rich context of human and ethical experience before one would be considered fully prepared. The true professional is not just someone with a job, but a person with a mission, a life's work through which one's highest humanity is expressed.

By searching for a new integration of liberal learning and professional preparation, we are not subverting the two traditions we have kept so far apart, but rather restoring the fullness of each. Breaking out of the little boxes of our sterile debates will help us move closer to helping our students become both true professionals with solid ground on which to stand and profess something, and truly liberally educated persons prepared to be and therefore to do. Liberal education and preparation for life's work desperately need each other. For just as liberal learning reminds us of the Socratic principle that "the unexamined life is not worth living," so experience teaches the complementary truth that the unlived life is not worth examining.

Today I am challenging Elmhurst College to assume a leadership position in this search. Because of the special heritage of this institution that emerged from the desire to prepare clergy and teachers, but always in the liberal arts tradition; because of Elmhurst's experience with excellent professional programs that have been well integrated into its overall mission; because of our rich mix of students—from traditional college-age students to adult commuters already in professional roles; because of our broad-ranging faculty, many with active professional lives outside of academe; and because we are already committed to providing students with the best of the liberal arts and the best professional preparation—because of these realities, this college is particularly well positioned to forge a fresh understanding of the true synergy between liberal learning and professional preparation. Even our physical setting, on a campus that combines an idyllic and protected space with ready access to world-class metropolitan resources, speaks to our unique potential.

So let us imagine a new reality, and then let us build it.

- Let us imagine a college that is so clearly focused on bringing together the strands of liberal learning and professional preparation in the experience of every student, whatever the program and whatever the level, that there is always a strong answer to the question, "What is special about Elmhurst?"

- Let us imagine a college where each academic program, indeed each course, challenges students to address the larger questions of meaning and purpose that have always been the marks of liberal learning, while also guiding students toward issues of application in their personal and professional lives; a college that takes a liberal approach to professional preparation and a professionally relevant approach to liberal studies.

- Let us imagine a college where all aspects of college life outside the classroom reflect this guiding principle, where there is a distinctive intellectual climate informed by this synergy, where focused student activities and physical fitness opportunities make it clear that this is not just another fun-and-games campus, but a place of serious and enthusiastic preparation for professional and personal lives of achievement and service.

- Let us imagine a college where the career-services function is a major component of the academic and intellectual life of the campus, where students begin to work toward their professional futures from the beginning of their college experience, where they have access to mentors who can help guide them and to experiences in significant work settings that can help give them a firm grip on the connections between theory and practice.

- Let us imagine a college where subjects we have traditionally associated with liberal education take on fresh life and vigor as students come to understand the place of such study in their lives; a college where the study of foreign languages is eagerly embraced, and where debates on questions of ethics and historical interpretation take on special intensity because the connections to life's dilemmas are constantly stressed.

In short, let us imagine a college that is a stronger and more vital liberal arts college because it is a place of true professional preparation, and a college that is also a more vibrant and distinctive place for professional preparation because it insists on being a place of liberal learning.

And then let us build on the strong foundation we have here at Elmhurst to create just such a college. The task before us is both conceptually and practically difficult, but it is a challenge worthy of our attention and energy. It is also an exciting prospect that will both stretch and energize us. I believe we will find significant help and encouragement from our friends and supporters, and I believe that many prospective students will respond with enthusiasm to such a college, convincingly described.

Almost exactly seventy years ago, H. Richard Niebuhr assumed the presidency of Elmhurst College. The struggling institution he and his colleagues nourished in this pleasant place has matured and grown strong. President Niebuhr once wrote that Elmhurst College seemed to him to be "an ever-widening circle," and it has continued to be so as it has developed new strengths and invited in new students. Now it is time to enlarge the circle in an intellectual sense as well, exploring new questions and developing a larger vision of what we can offer to the world.

I look forward with enormous enthusiasm to sharing this important work with you. There is so much excellence here and so much potential. We all know that there will be many demands on our energies and endless obstacles to overcome. But let none of them distract us from the challenge of the Royal Portal, the challenge to build doors of learning that bring together life's major elements into a coherent design of integration and integrity. I can almost hear Bishop Thierry and the designers and artisans of Chartres saying to us today, "We built to explain what was important to us, and we gave it our very best. Go now and build your own new portals. Just make them—as we did—true to your own time, to your own commitments, and to your own vision."

TWO

Becoming Newcomers

NEW STUDENT CONVOCATION
AUGUST 21, 2002

A large percentage of the people in this room had the experience today of stepping into a completely new home. Those of you who moved into a residence hall room went from that first moment when you opened the door to actually filling the space with personal belongings and settling down to live there in a matter of hours. Students who will commute from home also stepped into new spaces all around the campus today, spaces that will also come to feel like home over the weeks and months ahead. This ceremony is a time when the College symbolically puts its arms around its new students and says, "You are part of us now," but that won't stop you from feeling like newcomers.

The arrival of newcomers is nothing new here at Elmhurst College. It has been going on ever since our school first opened here in 1871. The very first arrival was on December 6 of that year, the date we celebrate as our founding date. Old-timers here know well the story of that inauspicious beginning. The church that wanted to sponsor a new school had been given some land—actually a small farm with a farmhouse that stood about where the Frick Center is now. They had tried to start a school in Indiana, but they couldn't make a go of it, so they decided to move the students and their teacher here to Elmhurst.

On that December day, Frederick Kranz, who was the entire faculty and staff of the school, arrived by train with fourteen boys, all German speakers, mostly recent immigrants. I am sure they were as excited as any newcomers as they stepped off the train at the Elmhurst station. But standing there on the platform, they discovered that the baggage car carrying all their possessions was missing. Their clothes, their books, and everything they needed to start a new school—had somehow gone astray. So the very first moment in our history consisted of the entire college stranded on the platform with absolutely nothing.

Now some of you parents who lugged refrigerators up to third-floor rooms might be intrigued by such an unburdened arrival, but the fact is they were really stuck. Well, it turned out that some folks in town put them up in their homes and a few weeks later the baggage just as mysteriously showed up, and the little band was able to move in and start classes.

As you process your arrival as newcomers and wonder if you will ever survive this really challenging experience, you might want to think back to your predecessors—strangers in a strange land, standing on that platform. At the very least, it's a reminder of how fortunate you really are. But more than that, the story of our beginning is a reminder that being a newcomer is an inevitable part of the experience of being a student. And I want to suggest that it goes even deeper than that. In a sense, education is all about becoming a newcomer. You may think that you have come here to learn a lot of things so that you won't feel like a newcomer any more, whatever you do in life. I would put it differently. You have come here to learn how to be a newcomer.

When you first learned to read, you read those simple stories over and over until the words became familiar and you could recognize them even when they weren't part of the story. But the whole point was to be able to read things that were new to you. Now, during your college years, I can assure you that you will have a great deal of opportunity to read things that are new to you. We are going to do our best to put you in positions where you will be a newcomer in the world of ideas. You will enter as a newcomer into subjects you have never before seriously studied. You will constantly find yourself studying, eating, playing, and participating in activities with new groups of fellow students. Some of the people who will meet you on the platform and guide you to those new intellectual spaces are sitting around you on the left and right. They are your professors, and as friendly and supportive as they are, you must understand that it is the job of the faculty to keep pushing you out of your comfort zone into new territory.

And what is the purpose of all this? This may not be the news you're looking for right now, but the point is to help you become really good newcomers. Good newcomers are curious and seek out opportunities to exercise their newcomer skills. They seek out new information, new ways to think about things, problems that haven't yet been solved. Good newcomers look around a lot, and because they have fresh eyes they see things others might miss. They do things like purposely sitting down for lunch with folks they don't know; they take trips to places they've never been to before; they try out activities they've never been involved with before; they surprise themselves and their friends by attending a lecture or a concert because there might be something new to learn.

And good, experienced newcomers have some very important skills and attitudes to take with them into their careers. They are ready to accept the new challenging assignment. They can analyze a market opportunity and imagine a creative new strategy. They can see into a societal need and envision how the world might be made a better place. They can change their minds when they learn new things that make them question old assumptions.

It would be easy to tell you not to worry about being a new-comer, that you'll get over it quickly and put it behind you. But the facts are more complicated than that. Sure, you'll feel at home here pretty soon and you'll have friends with whom you will become comfortable. But if Elmhurst College is successful with its plans for you, you will feel like a newcomer over and over during your time here, you'll get better and better at it, and for the rest of your life you'll continue to bring that attitude to everything you tackle.

So savor the experience of being a newcomer. Step back in your mind and consider how it feels. What are the hard parts about being a newcomer? What is painful? What helps? Who helps? What are you learning about yourself and about others around you? Then think of what you are going through as practice—practice for all the experiences ahead in which you will again have that feeling of being a newcomer. Don't get over being a newcomer; just get better at it.

And one more thing. If anyone here thinks I've been talking only to our recently arrived new students, you haven't been listening carefully. An old bit of folk wisdom says that you can never step into the same stream twice. None of us has been at this day, in this hour, before. Try looking at your world through the newcomer's lens, and you may see familiar things for the first time. A year's worth of new experiences and new learning lies ahead of us if we carry with us through the year the curiosity and the freshness of spirit that new beginnings inspire.

And so, with full confidence that we can build here in this place a company of scholars who share a passion for learning, I officially convene the 132nd academic year of Elmhurst College. May God bless our common enterprise and grant us—newcomers all—the wisdom to fulfill the potential of this year together.

THREE

We

NEW STUDENT CONVOCATION
AUGUST 20, 2003

This is the day when Elmhurst College reaches its collective arms around all who are new to our campus and says, "You are now—we." *We*: one of the English language's simplest words, yet one of the most powerful concepts in human history.

It's a word by which loving couples describe themselves, and a word that drives the success of huge corporate ventures. It appears prominently whenever effective leaders inspire others, from Winston Churchill's "We shall fight on the beaches, we shall fight on the landing grounds, we shall fight in the fields and in the streets, we shall fight in the hills; we shall never surrender," all the way back to the granddaddy of motivational speeches, Shakespeare's King Henry the Fifth, rallying his outnumbered forces on St. Crispin's Day at Agincourt in 1415: "We few, we happy few, we band of brothers." And for all Americans, what more telling example of the power of this little word could we have than its position as the very first word of the most important words we share as a nation: "We, the people."

The process by which people change from *you* and *they* to *we,* and sometimes back again, is one of the major themes in history and the social sciences. We, the people of the United States of America, have sometimes lost our "we-ness," most tragically in the Civil War. Conversely, the history of post-World War II Europe is a complex saga of nations, exhausted by killing each other, gradually finding their way to "We, the European Community." The challenge of leadership, whether political, corporate, or educational, is very largely a matter of creating an effective *we*. I am quite sure, for example, that the coaches who are putting you student-athletes through your paces these warm days are watching carefully to see if the team becomes *we* quickly enough to be successful in competition.

Today we say that all of you are *we*. Of course, saying so doesn't make it so. If simply declaring something could create reality, we would long since have had peace in the Middle East, a healthy economy, and a row of pennants flying above Wrigley Field. No, it will take some time for you to feel at home in your new surroundings and to feel one with your new colleagues—some time and probably some effort. But somewhere along the way, you will catch yourself talking to your parents or friends back home about something *we* are doing or how *we* feel about something and realize that you are including the rest of us in your *we*.

We is a comfortable feeling. It is a refuge from individual isolation, from homesickness, from fear of the unknown. But there is a more important reason for the *we* of Elmhurst College—an educational reason. There are probably some pieces of a college education you could have gotten sitting at home in front of a computer screen. But learning is only in part an individual process. The most profound learning invariably has a community context. We learn in interaction with other people—people who challenge us, inspire us, give us ideas, and polish our thinking in the daily give and take of conversation and argument.

So we are together for a reason. And here at Elmhurst, our *we-ness* is one of our most impressive strengths. It is particularly important to our college community that we are a small college, where we can actually get to know each other, where professors know the names of their students, where each of us can find the particular way that we can shine and make our special contribution. And I think newcomers will find as they get to know our college that folks around here tend to pay attention to *we*. It's why we try to take the time to help each other, to treat each other courteously, and try to fix problems rather than to lay blame. Even the little things make a difference. Every time we say hello to someone we pass on the sidewalk, or hold the door for someone coming after us, or pick up a piece of trash to keep our campus beautiful, we are reinforcing for ourselves and for others what *we* means on this campus.

We works only if we all assume some responsibility for making it work. We saw how this happens last week when the lights went out in New York and elsewhere. The next morning the papers were filled with examples of how people actually acted as though they were fellow human beings. Here's one from *The New York Times*:

> Christopher Davie, a hairdresser by profession, turned into a traffic cop at Eighth Avenue and 29th Street, one of the most nightmarish intersections in the city even during the best of rush hours. [As he helped traffic move through the bottleneck] some shouted "bravo!" to him. A grateful tourist from Montreal got out of her car and gave him a peach. Why did he do it? "There were ambulances trying to get through," Mr. Davie said. "Somebody had to get out here and do this."

As we praise examples of the *we* attitude and recognize the importance of this aspect of our life here at Elmhurst, we do need to remind ourselves that *we* can get complicated. The shadowy side of this powerful word is that togetherness can easily become an instrument of exclusion. In his book on human evolution, *The*

Third Chimpanzee, Jared Diamond tells of his experience in New Guinea with Neo-Melanesian, a relatively new popular language that has emerged from the Pidgin English shared by speakers of different native languages. In spite of its simplicity, Diamond writes, it can be a "supple" language that "lets one make some distinctions that cannot be expressed in English…. For example, the English pronoun 'we' actually lumps two quite different concepts: 'I plus you to whom I am speaking,' and 'I plus one or more other people but not including you to who I am speaking.' In Neo-Melanesian these two separate meanings are expressed by [completely different words]." It is the distinction between "We are in this together," and "We have decided you should leave the island." Diamond writes, "After I have been using Neo-Melanesian for months and then meet an English speaker who starts talking about 'we,' I often find myself wondering, 'Am I included or not in your "we"?'"

We cannot afford to have members of our College family asking, "Am I included or not in your 'we'?" So let's be attentive to whom we're calling *we.* Obviously, we will be in particular groups—a team, a class, a club—each with its separate sense of identity. But the world desperately needs people who embrace a *we* that crosses boundaries. We undermine our community when we join with others to ostracize or marginalize. We will truly learn from our diversity to the extent that we stop thinking of those who seem different as *they* and bring them into our personal understanding of *we.* And by doing so we will be practicing for the even more important challenge of becoming people who look out across the entire world with all its pain and all its promise and think *we.*

So here *we* are at Elmhurst College. Welcome all to a bright new year. With high confidence that we can build here in this place a true learning community, a company of scholars, I officially convene the 133rd academic year of Elmhurst College. May God bless our common enterprise, that we may fulfill the potential of this year together.

I BEGINNINGS

FOUR
The Keys to the Library

NEW STUDENT CONVOCATION
AUGUST 23, 2006

A warm welcome to everyone who is a part of this convocation, whatever room you happen to be in right now as we overflow across the campus, whatever your relationship to our college family—parent, grandparent, sibling, professor, administrator, staff member, musician, student leader. And the warmest welcome of all to our newest colleagues, members of what will become the great Class of 2010 and new members of the Elmhurst Life Skills Academy, who are such valued members of our family. By some combination of hard work and good fortune and providence we are at last together, and I think that calls for a rousing standing ovation.

Exactly a hundred years ago, the president of a small college in Maine wrote a short essay on the meaning and value of going to college. He called it the "Offer of the College," and here is how he summarized what you new students should expect to get out of college:

> To be at home in all lands and all ages; to count Nature a familiar acquaintance, and Art an intimate friend; to carry the keys of the world's library in your pocket, and feel its resources behind you in whatever task you undertake; to make hosts of friends…who are to be leaders in all walks of life; to lose yourself in generous enthusiasms and cooperate with others for common ends—this is the offer of the college for the best four years of your life.

So wrote William Hyde, the seventh president of Bowdoin College. The language of the essay is perhaps more 1906 than 2006, but the images are strong and on target. "To be at home in all lands and all ages": what a succinct way to capture the value of a global perspective and historical literacy. "To count Nature a familiar acquaintance": what a poetic way to think of science. "To lose yourself in generous enthusiasms": that is exactly what we are looking for from our football team and our student newspaper. And, my personal favorite: "To carry the keys of the world's library in your pocket."

In the interest of full disclosure, I need to admit to you up front that to me a library is the most inspired of human inventions, and I will be sorely disappointed if heaven does not turn out to be a superb and endless library. In fact a special piece of my own college experience involved the weight of important keys in my pocket. I went to a college where students performed much of the routine daily work, and my assignment was to be the live-in custodian of the building that housed the art and music departments. You can imagine what it meant to me, a music major, to lock the doors at ten o'clock at night and then have it all to myself—dozens of fine pianos, a gem of a concert pipe organ, and best of all, the music library, full of scores and an incredible collection of LP recordings. Through many late-night hours, that library opened up a whole world of music. For me, carrying the keys to the music library more than compensated for the hours of sweeping and dusting the job required.

I hope that you too, at some point before you leave this place, will have a love affair with the library. But when President Hyde spoke of "the keys to the world's library," I think he had in mind an idea that is bigger than the fine brick building, the books and electronic resources, and the knowledgeable and helpful staff that make up the A.C. Buehler Library on our campus. And the keys you carry today as you begin your college journey—the security card that gets you into your residence hall, or the keys to the car that gets you to campus, or the Jaypass that is the key to so much at our College—all those keys, as practical as they are, stand for something even more important.

The deeper truth is that today you hold inside of you the keys that really matter. The world's library—the enormous collection of opportunities for learning and connecting and contributing—is waiting for you. And the doors to that library will be unlocked by your curiosity, your hard work and growing competence, and your commitment to doing something with your life. Those are your keys to the world's library, whose doors are right here at Elmhurst.

So what's behind those doors? What has your college planned for you? What are our hopes and dreams and aspirations as we welcome you into our company of scholars? Well, we do have an agenda. We think you are great, we like what we know about you so far, and we're very glad you decided to be a part of our family. But the fact is, we'd like to change you. And here is how:

We want you to think more deeply. Our world so needs people prepared and willing to go beyond superficial thinking (or even no thinking at all), so we will work with you on researching, analyzing, evaluating, problem solving, discovering, and creating. For some reason we call it higher education, but its real goal is thinking deeply.

We want you to connect more broadly. We pursue truth by subject or discipline, but truth itself is not divided into separate disciplines. Crossing boundaries, reaching for broader perspectives, learning from diversity, and building on the breadth of a liberal arts education are ways we will help you connect broadly.

We want you to prepare to serve usefully. Elmhurst graduates make a difference, and helping you be ready to be a true professional in your chosen field, an engaged citizen, and a person experienced in both teamwork and leadership will help prepare you to serve others usefully.

We want you to live faithfully. The values you bring with you from home and church and school are a starting point, but clarifying and assuming personal ownership of your values and then keeping faith with them as you wrestle with life's dilemmas is the way to a responsible, accountable, and faithful life.

Everything we do here is tied in some way to preparing you to think deeply, connect broadly, serve usefully, and live faithfully. That's what we as a college want for you. But ours are not the only hopes and dreams and aspirations that are swirling around this campus today. Your parents, along with your teachers and even your friends, have helped you get to this day, and they as well have hopes and dreams and aspirations for you. If you'll excuse me for just a moment, let me speak directly to them.

Parents, what a great job you have done over all those years preparing your students for this day. And now there is one more thing they need from you. It's simple and obvious, but I know from personal experience as a parent that it can be so hard. You've certainly practiced for it often enough. Remember the day your child rode that bicycle for the first time without training wheels? And you ran alongside holding on to the seat just in case? And then you—let go? Well, today is one of the days you were practicing for. Years of experience with thousands of college students have taught me that your child's success in college depends to a significant degree on how well you pull off this most challenging of parental responsibilities. By all means keep in touch, and an occasional care package will certainly be appreciated, but riding a bike and learning to keep your balance is hard enough without having to drag a parent down the street. So—with love—let go. And students, sometimes it takes two to let go. Your parents have given you so much; give them a break now and help them with their big assignment.

So, new students, you have a lot of hopes and dreams and aspirations surrounding you today. We, the faculty and staff of Elmhurst, have an agenda for you, and goodness knows, your parents are not going to stop hoping and dreaming on your behalf. But remember those keys that you carry within yourselves? What matters now are your hopes and dreams and aspirations. And the keys that will open to you the world's library of opportunities to learn and grow are your own curiosity, your own effort, your own commitment to making a positive contribution to the world around you. Those keys are sacred and precious gifts. Now is the time to use them.

And so with high confidence that together we can become a true company of scholars, what college ought to be, I officially convene the 136th academic year of Elmhurst College. And I charge our newest students to remember always a special rule of our shared community here at Elmhurst College—a rule both profound and eminently practical: Don't lose your keys.

11 *Loving Learning*

FIVE

Dancing Along the Dingy Days

THE PRESIDENT'S BREAKFAST FOR
COMMUNITY LEADERS
MARCH 8, 1997

Welcome to the campus. We're delighted that you were able to accept our invitation to be here this morning.

There is a beautiful little phrase in the New Testament where the author of the Letter to the Hebrews speaks of the great "cloud of witnesses" that surrounds us—the people, past and present, who understand our struggles because they bear witness to their own. I have just that feeling on an occasion such as this, when a significant part of Elmhurst's very own cloud of witnesses has assembled in this room. You are the friends of the College who surround us, support us, cheer us on, sometimes give us the gift of constructive criticism, and in so many ways help us fulfill our mission as a college. This breakfast is at least one way for us to recognize this cloud of witnesses and to say thank you.

But I hope it is something else as well. This is an institution dedicated to education, and I hope you always have a sense, when you visit our campus, that you are touching base with learning, that in some sense you are reminding yourself of the central place of education in our human communities, and perhaps re-experiencing what education has meant in your own life. Just as you immediately have a feeling of special space when you step into a church, or a sense of history when you enter a carefully restored old building, I hope that when you come onto our campus, it feels like a special place where important things happen.

I'd like to talk with you a bit this morning about those important things, about the stuff of education. Now as some of you know, I have been speaking lately to people about the plans Elmhurst College has been developing for its future. The plans are indeed exciting, but they are not what I'd like to focus on today. You'll recognize that line as the classic approach of the politician running for office who begins every speech by saying that he certainly is not going to talk about his opponent's many faults, and he would certainly not dream of bringing up the subject of his opponent's several extra-marital affairs because he would not want to stoop to making his opponent's obvious immorality an issue in the campaign.

Well, I feel a bit like that when I say that I'm not going to talk this morning about the wide-ranging Action Plan we are developing or special elements of it. I will not discuss the new Center for Professional Excellence that is being designed to help all students move more effectively toward becoming true professionals in whatever field they pursue. And I won't talk this morning about the dream of a really fine performing arts facility on our campus that would bring the College and the community together for high-quality intellectual and cultural events. Rather than review our plans for the future and how we hope to implement them, I want to talk about what's behind it all.

And that is: what is taught and what is learned at Elmhurst College. Now the question of what *should* be taught—at all levels of our national system of education—is, nowadays, very much a part of the national discourse over education. As both our governor and our president have declared education to be at the center of their agendas, the question of what shall be taught turns out to be crucial. Should we adopt national standards to improve the probability that all students achieve a satisfactory level? But might that risk a one-size-fits-all approach that would push us toward a lowest-common-denominator definition of education? And so the debate will go.

And, of course, debates over what should be taught at the college level have been intense as well. In recent years, a steady stream of books, from *The Closing of the American Mind* to *Prof-scam* to, more recently, *The Opening of the American Mind* has brought to public consciousness a wide range of challenges and arguments about what is being and what should be taught in college. Should students be required to read the classics of our Western heritage—Plato, the Bible, Shakespeare—or should the emphasis be a broader range of the thinking of many cultures and more contemporary writing? Should college students prepare themselves specifically for the jobs and careers they will want to pursue after college or should they use their time at a more general level, reading widely and following special interests that will enrich their later lives?

One of the risks of trying to follow all of these arguments is that one might easily conclude that this is a new debate, that people didn't used to have to argue about such things. Implicit in many of the polemics for or against particular approaches to college education is the assumption that at some point in the past there was a golden age when it was done just right. If you have to take a guess, when you are listening to one of these arguments, it's a safe bet to assume that the golden age the speaker is imagining occurred just about the time he or she went to college.

The reality is that these debates have been going on for a very long time. Socrates was executed almost twenty-four hundred years ago because he took an unwavering and unpopular stand on the question of what and how the young men of Athens should be taught. The history of higher education is the history of disputes over what should be studied, and most of the changes have been hard-fought battles between preservers of a traditional way and advocates of a new revised curriculum, which a few decades later would itself be ardently supported as the traditional way. The Roman historian Livy, writing during the lifetime of Jesus, put it this way (and I will translate a little loosely): "Progress is a parade. When a man gets as far as he wants to go, he steps out of line and observes, 'Look at those damned radicals going by.'"

Indeed, the only condition that can truly be said to be traditional is change. Look at the curricular history of any old institution. The first students at Harvard College in 1636 took twelve courses over three years. About half of them were courses in ancient languages such as Greek and Hebrew. Latin was not included because a thorough knowledge was required for admission. Since those early years, the fights over the content of the curriculum have been brutal. In the early nineteenth century, Yale College was nearly torn apart when a teacher of Greek tried to get permission to use the writings of Homer in the study of Greek. Up until then only the New Testament was used for Greek instruction at Yale. The proposal was made even more radical by the fact that, since Greek was routinely taught on Monday, the college would be requiring students to study Homer, a pagan author, on Sunday. Some alumni were absolutely livid, the trustees got involved, and, as sometimes happens, the president tried to find a way out of the controversy by spreading the unhappiness as evenly as possible across the combatants. The professor was allowed to use Homer, but only as an option; he could not actually require his students to read it. Notice that this is the same Homer who was one of the cast of characters in the recent struggle over a Western-heritage program at Yale, except that by now almost nobody reads him in Greek.

My point is not that these constant debates over what should be taught were unimportant, but just that it is hard to find any period in which education satisfied everyone. Perhaps Aristotle captures it best. Here is a wonderful line from the *Politics*, written more than three hundred years before Christ: "At present, opinion is divided about the subjects of education."

So the debates of our day about what should be taught are very much in the ancient and honorable tradition. And they are fights that are very much worth fighting. I am not here today to propose solutions or to present the right answer. But in recent months, a feeling has been growing in my mind that I do want to share. I have been listening to a lot of views about what should be taught. Early in my time here I wrote to all our alumni asking for their views and got nearly six hundred responses. I meet regularly for breakfast with small groups of business and professional people and try to tap into their insights about what colleges should be teaching. And recently I had the privilege of serving on the task force that drafted a new strategic plan for District 205 and so I was a part of another set of discussions on the content of education.

Running through these many discussions has been a small thread. Most of the time it has been well concealed under talk of the need for computer expertise, for reading the classics, for studying foreign languages, for learning how to get along with others, and so on. But every now and then there have been little flashes when I think I have seen a glimpse of something usually missing in the lists of things students need. I have concluded that it is the missing link in most arguments about what should be taught, and that if we took it seriously, it would turn those debates into something much more fruitful.

A clue comes from something Albert Einstein once wrote. At one point a college in California asked him to compose a few words to inscribe on its new astronomy building. I would guess the school officials expected something grand about the incredible universe, or perhaps a prose version of the special theory of relativity. But he chose to celebrate something even more fundamental. Here is the motto he sent them: "It is the supreme art of the teacher to awaken joy in creative expression and knowledge."

"To awaken joy." What a stunning summary of what education is for, and how much it would breathe life into the sterile debates about course titles if we began with this basic premise. As I said, every once in a while it pops up. A few weeks ago, at a breakfast with a group of business leaders from the Elmhurst area, everyone was contributing to a growing list of things a good college should provide its graduates when one person who had been rather quiet said that he had just one thing to add. "I hope," he said, "that they will pick up somewhere the joy of learning." He went on to explain his view that the student who had experienced the joy of learning and knew something of how to find it had a big advantage both in making a living and in making a life.

I think that businessman was absolutely right, but I've been worrying about it ever since. And I am especially worried that, as hard as it has always been to help students feel the joy of learning, it's likely to become a good deal harder in the years ahead. We are entering a period of extraordinary change in the way information is processed, delivered, and spread around. We are on the verge of a period when enormous quantities of bits and pieces of information will be surrounding all of us all the time. There will be many wonderful outcomes of this revolution. But the ability to focus, to pay close attention to something long enough to love it, to select a few experiences of quality out of the universe of possibilities, will become extraordinarily challenging. The student trying to learn in the digital age is likely to feel like a teacup being filled with a fire hose.

So what are we to do—those of us who love learning and want Elmhurst College to be a place where the joy of learning is routinely awakened? I believe that some important pieces of an answer are here already. The simple reality of small classes with dedicated faculty who care about their students is so much a part of what we do that we sometimes forget how rare it is becoming in higher education and how important inspiring human contact can be. The willingness of the College to deal with issues of values and insist on an atmosphere of free and open inquiry is another component of the essential soil in which the love of learning can flourish.

But this is not just a matter of institutional policy. Each of us can do something much more personal. We can cultivate the joy of learning in our own lives and model it for others to see. Every time we discover a book that opens a new window for us; every time we take the initiative to sit in on a lecture or a discussion, especially one we think might challenge our own assumptions; every time we develop a new skill in something we love to do; every time we seek out and share with others a cultural event that enriches our lives, we are living out in a small way the joy of learning we want future generations to experience.

And so as I welcome you on campus and invite you to get in touch even if only briefly with the world of education at Elmhurst, let me offer you this thought—this vital and often missing piece of education—to take home with you. The debates you will hear, and participate in, about what should be taught to today's students are important. And they are likely to get even harder to resolve the further we move into the information age. But what ultimately matters at all levels of education is something that is captured in a beautiful and romantic way by the little poem printed on the back of this morning's program. The image of a simple man who discovers a book is about as far from most people's experience with the World Wide Web as you can imagine.

> *He ate and drank the precious Words—*
> *His Spirit grew robust—*
> *He knew no more that he was poor,*
> *Nor that his frame was Dust—*
>
> *He danced along the dingy Days*
> *And this Bequest of Wings*
> *Was but a Book—What liberty*
> *A loosened spirit brings.*

Unless we can capture the joy of learning that Emily Dickinson knew and infuse it into the experience of our students, the promise of the digital age will remain unfulfilled and the information superhighway will turn out to be nothing more than a long road of dingy days. Your support and encouragement are helping us in this important work, and I can wish for you nothing better in return than that you find many ways in the coming months and years to keep your mind dancing. Thanks for being here with us today and for all you have done—and all you will do—for Elmhurst College and its students.

SIX

The Spider and the Fly

THE PRESIDENT'S BREAKFAST FOR
COMMUNITY LEADERS
MARCH 4, 2000

The story is as simple as a morning stroll in the garden, as ancient as the early history of life on the planet, as contemporary as the Internet. Mrs. Spider, always looking ahead and anxious to preserve the ability of her fragile eggs to flourish in a future she will not see, has been up for hours getting ready for the dawn. With great care she has swung from branch to branch across the opening in the shrubbery, crisscrossing threads with just the right combination of suppleness and tensile strength. The design she is using, honed over the ages by her forebears, embodies principles it will take that young species, *Homo sapiens*, enormous mental effort to learn. But she creates it all as if in her sleep, and then retreats to a corner to wait.

Mr. Fly, equally intent on the long-term survival of his family line, has his own game plan, also passed on to him from his grandparents' grandparents' grandparents. Like Mrs. Spider's, his strategy has been enormously successful, statistically speaking. But it is quite different. No sitting around and waiting for Mr. Fly. The key is to attack the problem aggressively, to range over great distances to search out the bits of nourishment that will sustain his family. Success requires being on the move almost constantly in a risky dance of life. Mostly it works, but not always.

Just this morning, somewhere in your backyard or mine, this little fable was played out once again. On a pleasant day in early March of the year 2000, a fly headed for an opening in the shrubbery. In a sudden moment of truth in real time, two life strategies were tested against each other, and a bit of business was transacted on the web.

Mrs. Spider's web has become the metaphor of choice to identify a phenomenon that seems to be transforming our world right before our eyes. Like any good metaphor, the image of the web provides a flash of insight—and then goes on to suggest a set of more subtle propositions that help us ask useful questions. The World Wide Web is indeed a striking way to describe the radically new level of interaction we are now experiencing. But it also reminds us of an important paradox. To the spider, the web is a convenient tool for getting breakfast, a comfortable stroll to the convenience store down the street. To the fly, it is a deadly trap, a final lesson learned too late.

I want to use our brief time together this morning to reflect on the challenge of living in a time when we are experiencing the web of interaction in new ways. There are some big questions here—for all of us as individuals, for the communities in which we live together, and especially for the institutions of education on which we depend. Some of these questions can, I think, usefully be framed by that garden scene. How are *we* going to deal with the web of interconnectedness, of technology, of change, of uncertainty? And even more important to the people in this room—we who are gathered this morning because we value education—how are we preparing the next generation? Will they be spiders—using technology to live richer, fuller lives? Or will they be flies—trapped by their inattention to consequences and doomed to lose their freedom?

It is tempting to start with the hardware. Computers are important tools; people need to have them and they need to know how to use them. But that turns out to be the easy part. Of course, we have a long way to go, and the risk of leaving behind the have-not sectors of our communities is a serious one. But we know how to solve that problem. Indeed, the rapid spread of the equipment and the necessary skills is a good example of how societies learn. It's not the first time in history. People accommodated themselves to telephones and automobiles and steam engines and printing presses and firearms, all of which profoundly affected how people live and interact.

Clearly, the revolution we are experiencing goes beyond just computers. One might argue that the biggest change is the speed of change. I heard of a new research building that was dedicated recently at the Massachusetts Institute of Technology. A time capsule was placed in a prominent spot so that people in the future could look back, presumably on today's primitive technology. MIT plans to open that time capsule in five years.

At one level, we are becoming used to the idea of rapid change. It seems to be happening across a broad spectrum. Big businesses turning on a dime; advances in understanding subatomic particles and human genetics; the technical capacity to place scientific instruments on asteroids circling the earth and allow the committed day trader to make and lose money instantly on the New York Stock Exchange while sitting on a beach in Thailand—these things no longer surprise us.

But being jaded is not the same as understanding. We know intuitively that great leaps in technology will create trails of consequences, but we don't know what they will be. There are so many unknowns. What will be left of the enterprises we have known when the dust settles after the e-commerce revolution? What will our daily life be like when it is possible to work twenty-four hours a day with no time boundaries and with the cultural expectation that you are accessible whenever and wherever? How will it feel to know that every transaction in which we are involved leaves an electronic record we cannot control? How will we react when we have the technical prowess to do things we never thought we could do—things like selecting in advance the sex of our children or knowing now whether we will suffer from a debilitating disease in later life?

So many new things; so many new things to worry about. Life seems to be getting really complicated. Robert Kegan of Harvard University recently published a study of "the mental demands on modern life," and titled it *In Over Our Heads*. It remains to be seen, of course, whether that is really the case, whether human beings will ultimately have what it takes to handle all this complexity in our lives. But if we are to move forward and not be paralyzed, if we are to harness technology and use its power to enlarge our humanity, we will need to look carefully at how we learn and how we teach.

This is a question I believe we will be wrestling with well into the foreseeable future. What sort of educational goals, what sort of curriculum do we need, in this world of rapid and unsettling change, in order to keep our heads above water, to be able to be more fully human in the age of complexity? What is the curriculum of the spider? I want to suggest four things we need to learn and teach.

The most obvious starting point, and the easiest educational objective to achieve, is basic technical competence. In a world of machines, learn how to use the machines. Notice, though, that definitions of technical competence change over time. At the beginning of the automobile age, the skill set needed to drive a car emphasized basic mechanical skills with wrenches and screwdrivers. You needed to know how to adjust the spark advance and do field repairs with everything from oatmeal for leaky radiators to baling wire to hold things together. We still drive cars, but we don't really need to understand carburetors. We do, however, have to have the skills to pilot two tons of steel going eighty miles an hour with other cars coming toward us at eighty miles an hour and passing within inches. Intense attention and quick reflexes have replaced the skills of a hobbyist mechanic as the essential tools of the driver.

So technical skills that keep up with technology are a first step. But learning to use a computer—or the Internet or any other tool—is the easy part. Try to learn something by using the Web, and a whole new level of challenge becomes clearer. There's no shortage of bits of information, but how do you sort out what is reliable, what is misinformation, what is biased by its intent to sell you something? On the surface, the Internet seems to be an immense public library, but when you try to use it, you quickly find there's not a librarian in sight. And as you wander down the aisles, it begins to feel more like an exotic bazaar, full of fascination, confusion, and risk. What is called for more than ever is judgment.

This second part of the curriculum—judgment—deals with assessing quality. It suggests skills in interpreting statistics, in weighing evidence, in uncovering incompetence or deceit. What should you take seriously and what should you keep at arm's length? If anything will characterize the age of complexity, it will be the enormous responsibility placed on individuals to exercise such judgment. One of the first reactions to the invention of the printing press in the fifteenth century was fear on the part of religious leaders that ordinary people would read the Bible for themselves without the mediating influence of an authoritative clergy to tell them what to think. We are entering an era characterized by the absence of any apparent mediation. Helping people develop their own powers of judgment is an extremely important priority.

The first two goals of technical competence and the development of good judgment will take us and our students a long way. But a long way to where? The more we get into this new age of complexity, the more we will need to be able to get away from it. It is terribly important to have a critical perspective, to be able to stand back from what you are doing and ask what is really happening. The great violinist Itzhak Perlman tells of his first music teacher, who drummed into him this cardinal rule for achieving excellence as a musician: "Itzhak, Itzhak," his teacher would plead. "Listen to what you are doing, not to what you think you are doing." Perlman says it was the most important thing he ever learned.

This ability to be critical, to step away and listen carefully and evaluate what is going on, is a missing element in much of education. It is at the core of what we call liberal arts education. This tradition says, "Go out and be curious. Learn deeply and broadly about culture and society. But always be prepared to question. If you're beginning to feel comfortable, get suspicious. When you see prosperity, ask about social justice. While you are celebrating your freedom to get all sorts of information without filters, look carefully for the invisible filters and the ways you could be manipulated." For people of faith, religious commitment provides a ground to stand on when we need to step back and evaluate what is going on and what we are doing. Our values provide a template against which to measure what we see. This ability and willingness to exercise a critical perspective will be increasingly important as we negotiate complexity and rapid change.

So we have built an education around competence, judgment,

and critical perspective. But there is an honors course without which the rest of the curriculum is pointless. More than anything else in the emerging era, we will need—and our students will need—to choose the commitments that will drive us. What are our purposes in life? What is most important to us? James Barksdale is a business leader who has been enormously successful. Heading companies such as FedEx, AT&T Wireless, and Netscape, he has exemplified the vigorous, transforming leader. When asked recently the secret of his leadership, he said, with a rich Mississippi drawl I will not attempt to imitate, "The main thing is to make damn sure the main thing is really the main thing." That principle goes for a lot more than just making a profit for your company. The best hope we have for keeping technology in perspective is to keep ourselves clearly focused on whatever is for us the main thing.

What are *your* main things? What are the most important things in your life? What are the goals that drive you? Is your family at the core? Then by all means use technology to help your family stay close and to create opportunities to grow together. But make damn sure the main thing stays the main thing. We can reasonably predict that staying focused on worthy goals will be both harder and more important in the years ahead.

So we have technical competence, good judgment, a critical perspective, and firm commitment to worthy goals. These are the things that will help us approach life in the age of complexity as spiders rather than flies. These are the things education must be about. These are the things we try to be about at Elmhurst College. But these are also the things communities ought to be about. If the Internet is teaching us anything, it is the interdependence of people. The social web that unites us as a community here in Elmhurst means that the welfare of each of us is inextricably tied to the welfare of all of us. When we consider decisions like a referendum to lift up the education of children, we need not ask whose children. They are all our children. They are our future. The children of District 205, the students at Elmhurst College, and all of us in this room are entering a new era—a time rich in potential and full of risk. Nothing is more important at this point than learning and growing as people, and nothing we can do will reach out and touch the future like supporting the learning and growth of those who will follow us.

Mrs. Spider is resting comfortably in your backyard right now. She's had a good breakfast, and her little ones are secure for today. But she'll be back on the web tomorrow, focused intently on what needs to be done. We've had a good breakfast as well, and it's time to return to the chores and the joys of a fine Saturday in March. Let us take with us a renewed commitment to thinking carefully about our world, to learning every day for the rest of our lives, to assuring the very best education possible for all the students around us, and for keeping the main things the main things in our lives.

SEVEN

Only Connect

These few weeks at the end of our calendar year have come to mean many different things. It is a time of frenetic activity, but also a time when we savor occasional moments of quiet and peace. It is a time to remember important events in our faith traditions, and it is a season of extreme materialism. It is a time to recall one little child who changed the world, and it is a time to pay attention to all our children and to what one generation can give another. It is a time to celebrate and a time to reflect. Some of my reflections, in this year of unresolved conflicts and an unfinished election, have been about connections.

E. M. Forster was an English novelist of the early twentieth century. Some of his best-known books have been made into movies, and many people have come to know him through *A Room With a View* and *A Passage to India*. Forster was a keen observer of the human condition and of the impact of changing technology, and he saw that with automobiles and telephones and competitive businesses and hectic cities, our lives become more and more fragmented. We are pressed to act in so many different arenas that we lose an overall guiding perspective. In Forster's novel *Howards End*, we meet the cultured and sensitive Margaret Schlegel and Henry Wilcox, the older, pragmatic businessman she eventually marries. What troubles Margaret about Mr. Wilcox is his inability to see beyond his business interests to the romance of life, which he has buried inside himself. Here is Forster's description of the challenge Margaret faces:

> Mature as he was, she might yet be able to help him to the building of the rainbow bridge that should connect the prose in us with the passion. Without it we are meaningless fragments, half monks, half beasts, unconnected arches that have never joined into a man…. [I]t was here that Margaret hoped to help him.

And here is Forster's description of what Margaret sets out to teach Mr. Wilcox:

> Only connect! That was the whole of her sermon. Only connect the prose and the passion, and both will be exalted, and human love will be seen at its height. Live in fragments no longer. Only connect, and the beast and the monk, robbed of the isolation that is life to either, will die.

Margaret learns, of course, how risky it is to enter into marriage actually believing we will be able to change our spouse. That's something I guess most of us learn in one way or another. But the fact that Margaret was only partly successful in her attempt to remake her husband does not alter the subtlety and the significance of her message. For Forster, it became the central theme of the novel, and when *Howards End* was published in 1910, the frontispiece carried the simple motto: "Only connect …."

Much of our learning and growth as people can be understood as a process of making connections. As infants, we begin to connect the strange sounds people around us make with particular things and actions, and thereby discover the joys of language. In school we read Shakespeare in one course and study history in another and, if we are lucky, have some of those rare "Aha!" moments when we realize that those two different things are actually connected. Early on most of us develop a capacity to spot inconsistencies in other people's behavior. When we believe they are saying one thing but doing something else, we learn to call them hypocritical. When we feel a parent or teacher is treating us differently from the way a sibling or classmate is being treated, we cry out, "That's not fair!" So eventually we come to know at least something of what connection feels like and what happens when other people fail to connect their theory and their practice.

But then we grow up and life stretches out, and making connections becomes much harder. In a world of almost infinite options, we must specialize. So we proceed in our education and learn more and more about less and less. We respond to the busy blur of life around us by blotting most of it out so that we can get on with the practical necessities.

At one point in *Howards End*, Forster writes about a difficult morning after Margaret has made a valiant effort to help Henry Wilcox learn to connect:

> But she failed. For there was one quality in Henry for which she was never prepared, however much she reminded herself of it: his obtuseness. He simply did not notice things, and there was no more to be said. He never noticed…the lights and shades that exist in the greyest conversations, the [guide]-posts, the milestones, the collisions, the illimitable views. Once—on another occasion—she scolded him about it. He was puzzled, but replied with a laugh: "My motto is Concentrate. I've no intention of frittering away my strength on that sort of thing." "It isn't frittering away strength," she protested. "It's enlarging the space in which you may be strong." He answered: "You're a clever little woman, but my motto's Concentrate." And this morning he concentrated with a vengeance.

One of the great challenges we all face is how to connect the pieces of our lives. We are pulled in all sorts of directions and hustled along by the frenetic world around us, and it sometimes feels as though if we were actually to pull ourselves together and stop to smell the roses, we would immediately be rear-ended by the huge truck of all our commitments. Henry Wilcox's solution seems the only viable choice. Concentrate, focus, resist distraction. Lord, give me the chance to do just one thing well.

And yet it turns out that concentrating with a vengeance is not always the shortest road to fulfillment. One of the ironies of our age is that just as our scholarly and scientific disciplines have become hyperspecialized, we are discovering that creativity and excitement are often found at boundaries between disciplines. The real breakthroughs are more likely to come when an investigator makes a connection across boundaries. It is when the apparently unrelated turns out to be the missing piece that the next step toward understanding becomes possible. What society needs is people who have developed appropriate special competence but who haven't stopped there, people with broad interests and wide perspectives, people who can relate pieces of their experience with other pieces, people who can see the connections.

And this is not just a matter of intellectual bridge building. It extends as well to how we connect our purposes and our practice. What we hope for our children—and what we need ourselves—is the ability to take our dreams, our values, and our ideals and connect them to our daily actions in our work, in our families, and in our communities. This is the sort of integration between prose and passion that makes us whole people. It's no accident that when we see people who are able to connect the fragments of their lives we say they "have their act together."

So Forster's motto is a reminder on the importance of internal connectedness—the capacity to bring together the various pieces of our experience, to keep broadening our understanding, and to connect the ideals we want to live by with all the things we do and the choices we make each day. But there is, as well, a second sense in which Margaret's little sermon might open a window to new perspectives. Connectedness is not just a matter of internal integration; it is also the stuff of which social life is made. Our times call not just for whole people, but also for whole communities.

Indeed, I think it is fair to assert that the issue for the twenty-first century is whether we as human beings can learn to connect across the lines of difference that divide us from each other. Our lives together, our families, our neighborhoods and cities, our civic culture, the quality of the world we leave our children all demand that we get better at understanding people who are different.

And of all the tools we have to build bridges across the barriers that divide, the simplest and most effective is human connection. Reaching out to the stranger, to the person who looks and acts different, to the person with a way of thinking we don't understand, even to the person we don't much like—only by someone reaching across the boundaries of hurt or strangeness or fear can connections eventually be made. The cynic will say all this is naïve; the realist will understand that there is simply no other way. If we are to build strong families, healthy communities, and a safer world, E. M. Forster's motto challenges us to take the necessary first step: only connect.

When I submitted the title of these remarks to be printed in the program, I had no idea we would, as a nation, still be debating a decision we all thought would be clearly made on November 7.

One of the striking things about the past few weeks has been the extent to which those involved in the struggle have positioned themselves on one side or the other of a great divide. We've heard a lot of sports metaphors, and one image that comes to mind is half the country on one side of the football field, the other half on the other side, with the only interaction taking place on the field between them. It's Harvard on one side, Yale on the other, connected only by collisions on the field or the exchange of verbal taunts from the stands. Sportsmanship is in short supply, and it turns out even the officials on the field are alumni of either Harvard or Yale. Perhaps many of us don't view ourselves as noisy fans in this image, but there we are, and no one at the game, it seems, can rise above partisanship.

Well, we simply have to get through these days, let the game play itself out and trust that somehow we'll at least be able to have a drink together afterward. But the experience ought to remind us once again what a daring thing it was to name this country the United States of America. It has never been easy to create and sustain united communities. And when the long count is over and we hear the words "So help me God," there will still be the same challenge that we have always faced—building a workable community over lines of difference. Those who would represent us in Washington or Springfield or Elmhurst could do worse than start every day by reminding themselves: only connect. And each of us will have a chance to cast another vote in this strange election by walking across the field after the game and shaking hands with someone who thinks otherwise and declaring our interdependence.

The world needs people who can connect the fragments of their lives and approach the wholeness God intended, and people who are able and willing to connect with others and work toward wholeness in society. Producing such people is exactly what Elmhurst College has been doing for 129 years. The special characteristics of our college all speak to this commitment:

- A liberal arts education that develops the capacity to make connections across a broad swath of knowledge.

- Preparation for professional life that helps graduates connect the way they make a living to the values with which they strive to make a life.

- An active service-learning program that connects students to people they can help and gives them the experience of what it means to give back to one's community.

- And, at a basic level, the human scale of our small college that puts dedicated professors and small classes of students together in daily rituals of intense connection.

This evening, we in this room are connected with one another by our devotion to a great college. Throughout its history, Elmhurst has been carried along and nurtured by a host of people who have cared about its mission and its students. There have been people who stepped forward to assume leadership when the institution seemed fragile and patiently built up its strength—people like Ivan Frick. There have been people who signed on to help the College not as alumni or as employees but simply as friends, people who found something here worth supporting and defending—people like former Board Chair Lloyd Palmer and Jack Kelly. There have been people who found Elmhurst and put down roots here and flourished and became exemplars of the tradition, great teachers whose influence continues to nourish students throughout their lives—people like Dr. Rudolf Schade. And there have been many, many students who learned and grew here and went on to make something of their lives, while never forgetting their debt to their alma mater—people like Les and Joan Brune.

So tonight we remember and honor the ties that bind us. And tonight Elmhurst College says to each of you: Thank you for all you have done to assure that our students of today and tomorrow will experience the best possible Elmhurst College. As you celebrate the season, may you, this year, find special joy in connection—the connections that make your life worth living, the connections that you can make with a world in need, the connections that help you understand, and the connection you discover with the grace and truth, which lie beyond our understanding.

Setting the Table

THE PRESIDENT'S HOLIDAY DINNER
DECEMBER 5, 2004

O ne of the special memories of my childhood is one I wonder if anyone else here shares. Much of our family life seemed to center around meals, and my siblings and I were assigned chores in turn—clearing the table, washing up, drying and stacking the dishes. But setting the table was my favorite assignment, probably because there was the least risk of breaking something and it meant you weren't stuck in the kitchen after the meal. On the special occasions of holiday feasts or Sunday dinner with company, there was the added attraction of bringing out Mother's good silver and lining up those shiny Fairfax knives, forks, and spoons, making sure there was the correct number of places around the table. At the time, we children were certainly not into psychological analysis, but looking back, I understand now the sense of shared responsibility for the family enterprise that those simple chores engendered.

Whatever your own memories of the meals of childhood, there is a good chance they still help shape the way you approach the dinner table today. That is at least one of the meanings of the old Italian saying, "At the table you don't grow old." And just as the experience of sitting down to a table set for a meal is one of the basic pleasures of life, so preparing the table for family or friends is an act of special affection. When the psalmist wanted to capture God's extravagant love in an image everyone would understand, he wrote, "Thou preparest a table before me…my cup runneth over."

For as far back as humankind can remember, sitting around a shared feast has meant more than just satisfying animal hunger. The ancient Greeks built a whole tradition out of food and drink as the catalyst for intellectual exchange. For Socrates and his friends, the best possible evening was a *symposium*—the word literally means "drinking together"—a shared meal that was the stage for the richest of conversations.

Special meals and their environments can have long afterlives, as we carry their memories in our hearts. Ernest Hemingway's memoir of his early years as a poor but happy writer wandering the cafés of Paris in the 1920s begins with these words: "If you are lucky enough to have lived in Paris as a young man, then wherever you go for the rest of your life, it goes with you, for Paris is a moveable feast."

An interesting way to think about a college education, isn't it? A feast you take with you for the rest of your life. And what a challenge for those of us who set the table and manage all the other chores of preparing that feast. All of the issues we struggle with as a college come down to the problem of creating a meal that is truly nourishing, truly sustaining, and truly memorable. What will be on the menu? Who will be invited to the table? What are their special needs? How can we blend healthy nourishment and appealing presentation for both short-term and long-term satisfaction? What shall we talk about, what is our intellectual agenda, and how do we guide the conversation around the table for the best benefit of all? How do we inspire our guests to leave the banquet fired up to make a positive difference in the world? And, of course, inevitably, where will the resources come from, and how will the grocery bill be paid?

All of you in this room have been involved in one way or another with just these issues. As we have worked together to build the Elmhurst College of today, each of you has brought something distinctive to the table. And now here we are, around the dinner table, as we celebrate another year together and especially the completion of a major capital campaign. So much has been accomplished during the years we have been working to put Vision In Action. In many ways the College has been repositioned and reenergized, and we are meeting even the challenges of a tight economic environment from a position of strength. But with all these successes, it is a good time to ask just what we have been creating. What sort of table have we set, and what is the nature and quality of the feast to which we invite our students?

In fact, the distinctive dimensions of the institution are emerging more clearly precisely because of the progress we have made in recent years. There are five big things to understand about our college. Think of them as five commitments we have made, five promises to the students we serve, five ways we shine. Or, if you want to think of an image from the season, they are five points of a very bright star.

First, Elmhurst College is committed to *education on a human scale*. We promise our students they will learn from a few great people whom they will get to know very well. We do not promise hundreds of professors, tens of thousands of fellow students, or an infinite number of courses from which to choose. We have decided to be a small college, and this issue of scale is one of our most important strengths and one of our toughest challenges. It means that in everything we do, we concentrate on the personal connection with each individual student. Classes are kept small, activities are kept accessible, advising and mentoring are individual processes. Our aim is to be, in Cardinal Newman's phrase, an alma mater who knows her children one by one.

Elmhurst shines in its personal attention and close human interaction. But maintaining that approach will always be a challenge in a culture that values and rewards the efficiency of large-scale institutions. I sometimes think of this matter of scale as the challenge of carving a cameo. How do we achieve extraordinary quality at the individual level while still keeping our costs to students manageable? Sometimes a piece of the answer may be to become a bit larger in some dimension, but underneath, the purpose is always so we can be even better at the personal level. Many of the questions about our future center on this matter of a human scale and how we can continue to make it work for us. How big should we become? How should we use technology? It all comes down to what will best enhance close personal relationships.

The second big commitment is to *liberal arts education*. For the ancient Roman orator Quintilian, the outcome of a true education was a good person, able to speak persuasively, capable of addressing any topic and assuming any position of leadership. That was what *artes liberalis*, the arts of the free man, the learning appropriate for the liberated person, was all about. If we have allowed this approach to learning to seem like fluff you study when you don't know where you're going, it is because we have lost the sense of purposefulness and significance the founders of the tradition assumed. Liberal learning is at the heart of our enterprise because it reaches for the richness of understanding that is humanity at its best. And the products of studying broadly and deeply—analytical thinking, effective communication, problem solving, connecting across boundaries, and judgment in the paradoxes of life—these are in fact the most practical of assets.

Liberal learning shines at Elmhurst, but continuing to achieve these objectives in a rapidly changing world is a challenge that won't go away. Sustaining the fundamentals that endure, addressing new realities that change things profoundly, using new tools to probe more deeply, all the while constrained by strict limits of time and resources, will require attention, discrimination, creativity, and an attitude of openness that accepts that there is always "more to understand."

Our third big commitment is to *professional preparation.* The work each of us does in the world is a major way we express who we are. But true professionalism is a high calling indeed. The particular skills of the job may seem like challenge enough. Elmhurst seeks to assure, through carefully designed disciplinary programs and through shining special opportunities such as the Center for Professional Excellence, that students come to understand that integrity, service to one's community, broad perspectives, and thoughtful attention to the impact of one's profession on other people are just as important.

Staying at the cutting edge of rapidly changing professions will be a real challenge for Elmhurst College in the years ahead. There is in fact a major role for folks just like you, professionals who can contribute by mentoring students and providing specialized advice about changes in your professional worlds.

Our fourth commitment is to *engagement in the world.* We are not just about bright students becoming individually successful. The point of making a difference in the lives of students is so that they can make a difference in the world. We want to push students out of their comfort zones and into the world, with all its challenges and opportunities for learning and for service. One of the biggest hurdles we face is the parochialism of our students, which in large part simply reflects the culture in which they grew up. When they take off on an international experience or find new friendships with people very different from themselves, they are stepping closer to the global perspective they will need in the years ahead.

Engagement may take many forms—civic engagement in the public arena, engagement with the natural world in scientific literacy and environmental stewardship, and engagement in the social struggles of our era. The job the College must undertake here is particularly challenging and increasingly urgent.

And finally, our fifth big commitment is to *values and ethics*. Perhaps a clearer phrase these days would be judgment and personal commitments, because the issue is so much deeper than values perceived as simply being on one side or another of questions on the popular agenda of the moment. We want our graduates to have thought about the profound dilemmas of the human condition—the alternative attractions of individualism and community, the inevitable tension between liberty for all and justice for all, the enormous distance they will find between peoples of different cultures and traditions. We want our graduates to have some sense of the ground on which they stand and the principles on which they want to build their lives and careers.

We value our heritage in a faith tradition characterized by respect for diverse perspectives, the search for peace, and a passion for social justice. But we are not a sectarian institution. We do not expect students to come with a particular set of answers. We do, however, want them to bring all of their questions and a willingness to listen, to think, to debate, to wrestle, to rethink, and to hone that rare quality we sometimes call wisdom. Most importantly, we hope they will understand this as the task of a lifetime, not a simple or final list of dos and don'ts. Elmhurst shines when our students progress in their journey of discovery and insight, framed by the message carved into Alumni Circle: "There is more to understand: Hold fast to that as the way to freedom."

So here you have five big things about your college, five things today's students are finding at Elmhurst, five shining points—a personal scale, liberal learning, professional preparation, engagement in the world, and values to live by. That is the feast for a lifetime that you are helping to provide for the next generation.

But there is something more subtle about setting a table that I don't want to rush past. On the surface, eating a meal may seem like a one-way process of moving food from one location to another. That's the simple model behind the old medieval couplet,

The tables groan before the feast,
The feasters groan thereafter.

True enough as far as it goes (though I hope there is only pleasant groaning here tonight). But preparing for the best of feasts means much more than just assembling some food. If it is to be a meeting of the minds as well as the stomachs, if there is to be food for thought as well, if there is to be a symposium around the table, then there is another sort of preparation to consider. As is often the case, a wise poet, such as Emily Dickinson, invites us to think more deeply. She writes:

Who goes to dine must take his Feast
Or find the Banquet mean—
The Table is not laid without
Til it is laid within.

So just as Elmhurst College invites its friends and supporters to join in setting the table for our students, it also invites us all to lay the table within and to make each of those five dimensions of Elmhurst a part of our daily lives as well. That is the way the

College will become a learning opportunity for all of us and we will truly join in its mission and make it our own. So let us make these five commitments:

Let us attend to the human connections in our personal circles of family and friends, remembering that the true measure of our success is not the wealth we have amassed but the gifts of caring, respect, attention, and intimacy we have given.

Let us seek breadth and depth of learning in our own lives, reading widely, following our curiosity, enjoying the richness of our culture and the diversity of the human experience, remembering that every answer has hidden in it an even more interesting question.

Let us aim at the highest professionalism in all our work, remembering our profound calling to be, in St. Matthew's words, workmen worthy of our meat.

Let us seek new ways to engage the world, to think and act as citizens with a global perspective, remembering the hazards of parochialism and the tragedy of family feuds of whatever scale.

And let us examine our own choices and our commitments to justice and compassion and service, always remembering the sneaky serpent of self-righteousness.

Because it turns out that the five big things about Elmhurst College are indeed five big things, a hearty meal for all. As we move into this holiday season, as we reflect on our great gifts from God, may all the tables we set and the feasts we share bring us closer to those we love and to the center and source of our being. And may the spirit of this simple prayer remind us of the Divine Guest who enriches every meal and every day:

Be known to us in breaking bread,
But do not then depart;

Savior, abide with us, and spread
Thy table in our heart.

Thank you all for being at our table here this evening and for your friendship and support of Elmhurst College and its students. And our very best wishes for the happiest of holiday seasons.

III *Interesting People*

NINE

The Space Above the Pillars

COMMENCEMENT ADDRESS
FEBRUARY 11, 1996

I t has become commonplace to observe that college graduates of today are likely to experience several different careers during their working lives. Indeed, one of the special challenges faced by higher education is how to help students be ready for a wide range of opportunities, some of which may not even yet exist. Some of you graduating today are here precisely because you want to move into a new career. But it would be wrong to believe that human versatility is new, or that doing a series of different things in one's lifetime is only a recent phenomenon. History is full of fascinating individuals who moved freely across boundaries that seem, in our era of specialization, almost insurmountable.

One of the most remarkable examples of such career flexibility was Christopher Wren. We remember Wren as England's most famous architect, but he began his professional life as a mathematician and astronomer. Born in 1632, he was appointed Gresham Professor of Astronomy at Oxford when he was only twenty-five and quickly moved to the leading edge of the science of his time. His work included significant advances in understanding the planets and the development of new ways to grind hyperbolic lenses for telescopes. From time to time, he was asked to undertake projects where his skills in drafting and geometry would be useful—redesigning a university building or devising fortifications for a harbor. As a scientist, he took professional pleasure in analyzing the forces and stresses that make buildings strong and serviceable.

The Great Fire of 1666 changed everything. Suddenly London was in ashes, and new opportunities opened. Within days, Wren presented a comprehensive plan for a new city—a plan soon rejected as too daring and costly. But architectural commissions followed, and by the time of his retirement, more than fifty churches and many other public buildings bore the mark of his graceful and often technically ingenious design. We know him best for the great Saint Paul's Cathedral, an extraordinary building where he was eventually buried in a plain tomb with a Latin inscription that reads *Si monumentum requiris circumspice*—"If you seek his monument, look around you."

Throughout his career, Wren fought a battle that professionals in many fields and in different eras will recognize. He knew what he was doing, but the people who used his services were not always convinced. His constant struggles with his patrons were not only on matters of artistic judgment. With some frequency, his careful calculations led to designs the authorities could not believe would work. There is a striking example of this in the Guildhall at Windsor. Just below Castle Hill, this is a building that served as the center for much of civic life—a sort of town hall for Windsor. It had been begun by another architect, and Wren was called in to complete the work. The main chamber was to be on the second floor, with space for an open-air market below. The upper part of the building would be supported by stone columns around the perimeter, and Wren planned the ceiling of the market area to span the entire footprint of the building with a large open area in the center. Tradition has it that the Guildhall council was appalled by the design and insisted that additional pillars would be required to carry the weight of the ceiling and the second story. Wren's experience and his calculations told him otherwise, but he was unable to get his design approved.

Reluctantly, he added the pillars. But compromising on a design was one thing; his integrity as a scientific architect was something else. So the four inside pillars were indeed built, ostensibly to keep the second floor from collapsing to the ground. But Wren and his builders knew that the columns were actually short of the ceiling by an inch or two. They are sturdy columns that to the casual eye appear to carry the weight above them, but they were intentionally made just a bit short. Wren knew his ceiling would safely span the distance he had originally planned, and he was determined to prove it—even if only to himself. We don't know whether the Guildhall council ever noticed, but we do know that the space above the pillars is still there, three hundred years later.

I'd like to focus our attention for a few moments not so much on the short pillars themselves as on that small space above the pillars. After all, the important thing was not that the pillars were too short to reach the ceiling, but that the ceiling was built a little higher and a lot stronger than it needed to be. What might we learn from the space above the pillars?

It may startle you to have gone through all those years of effort to complete your college education, only to be presented with a graduation address about nothing more than a little bit of air. But I want to suggest that, in the long run, we—as people and as professionals—will be known by the space above the pillars that we build. We will be known by our ability to go beyond appearances, beyond the requirements of our assignment; by the ways we apply our expertise and our energy above and beyond what people expect.

How often have we listened to a great musician or watched

a superb athlete in action and heard from a companion—or said ourselves—"excellent." In that simple exclamation is embodied half of the principle of the space above the pillars. To *excel* is to go a step beyond, to add that special twist of creativity, that particular polish that comes only from endless hours of practice.

But the other half of the principle is more subtle. There is a private dimension to the space above the pillars. It has to do with the excellence we strive for even when we know it may never be observed. It has to do with private, personal standards that are above those required by our public position. It is what we do when we are aiming to *be* rather than to *seem*.

What is needed if we are to do our work and live our lives with space above the pillars? Competence, certainly. Wren did not design the Guildhall ceiling with careless bravado. His calculations were the result of a lifetime of devotion to learning how buildings work. The competence you take with you from your formal education and sharpen with experience over the years will be an indispensable tool for building with excellence.

But beyond competence, wisdom is required. Wisdom is, perhaps, an old-fashioned concept. But how much we need today people who can see beyond the technical, beyond the simplistic ideological mind-set, beyond the biases and boxes that keep us from understanding things whole!

To competence and wisdom we must add purpose. Our College's statements of Mission and Vision speak of humane values, and unless we commit ourselves to such values—to justice, to compassion, to integrity—we risk building pillars that do nothing more than prove we can build pillars.

And, finally, there is, woven through all these requirements, one more thing. I'm sorry to have to bring this up, after all the effort you have put into getting to this moment of graduation, but ahead of you lies—more work, lots of it. There will be the extra late night hours needed to work on the project that will turn around your business or contribute to your profession. There will be the inconvenient demands of family and friends who will need you to be there for them just when it would be much easier to be somewhere else. There will still be, as there have been for years now, the hours of study and learning as you struggle to keep ahead of new knowledge and new challenges. Through it all you will need the simple discipline of hard, sustained work. As one careful observer of life has noted, the important work of the world is not done by those who sleep when they are tired.

And so as we examine the space above the pillars, it becomes clear that the essential elements in the formula are the same old fundamental ones we have wrestled with throughout our lives. And when we think back across our best experiences—our best memories from childhood, the best things we have learned from our friends, our best experiences in the world of work, the best gifts of challenge and encouragement we have received from our teachers—our best experiences have in fact been those that have nurtured precisely the qualities of competence, wisdom, purpose, and discipline that we need to become master builders of short pillars.

This commencement marks for each of you graduates the beginning of another stage in your life. Your work at Elmhurst has opened the door to new challenges and new successes. Your alma mater wishes you well as you walk through that door. May you find your place among those who value truth above power, wisdom above technical skill, compassion above competition. May the buildings you build be strong and beautiful. And may there be many, many times when you have the chance to build a little better than you need to, so that above some of the pillars that are required, there will be that special space, that secret signature that marks your work and your life as excellent. Congratulations to you all.

TEN

Let It Shine

NEW STUDENT CONVOCATION
AUGUST 24, 2005

T his summer an old man died in South Africa. He had almost no money, he had about a sixth-grade education, and according to the records, he was a retired gardener. He had lived much of his adult life in a one-room shack without electricity or running water. Why, then, did his obituary appear in *The New York Times*, *The Boston Globe*, and *The Economist*?

It's a fascinating story that is both inspiring and troubling. Hamilton Naki was born in a small village, where he received the meager education that was available. At age fourteen, he hitchhiked to the city of Cape Town to look for work. The job he found was at the University of Cape Town, where he was hired as a groundskeeper. After ten years caring for gardens and tennis courts, he was asked to help out in the medical department's animal laboratory, cleaning the cages and looking after the animals. As he later put it, "Nobody wanted to work with the animals as it was so dirty."

But what he saw in the lab was also intriguing, and little by little, Naki took on new tasks. He began helping with administering anesthesia and became a handy person to have about the lab. At the time, some interesting work was being done there exploring organ transplant techniques in animals, and Naki watched as he was helping out. When asked later how he learned so much about the practice of surgery with no formal education, he said simply, "I stole with my eyes."

Before long, he was experimenting a bit on his own after hours and practicing the techniques he had observed. Medical students learned that they could rely on him to finish up, quietly, an operation they had begun. Over the years, he became a repository of experience as students and faculty came and went. Eventually he was recognized within the lab as something of an expert, especially on intricate liver transplants in pigs that required extraordinary delicacy in joining tiny blood vessels.

Of course, the research with animals was aimed at helping humans, and so it was not a surprise to the medical community that the first successful human heart transplant happened in Cape Town, South Africa. All that research and experience came together in 1967, when Dr. Christiaan Barnard led a large team through the complex and daring surgery that implanted a human heart in Louis Washkansky. Stories differ on just what role Hamilton Naki played in the actual procedure, but he had certainly been a significant contributor to the years of preparation for that moment. There is, however, no mention of Naki in the press releases from that period.

Because the other side of the story of Hamilton Naki was the context of apartheid—the brutal system that kept races separated and whites on top. As a black man, Naki could not have gone to medical school, and he would certainly not have been legally permitted to participate in an operation on white people. As he later said, "I was one of the backroom boys. They put the white people out front. If people [had] published pictures of me, they would have gone to jail. They pretended I was a cleaner. It was the way things were." Officially, Naki never rose above the rank of laboratory technician, the highest assignment the university would give to someone with no degree.

But years later, after the collapse of the apartheid system,

Christiaan Barnard himself acknowledged Naki's significance. "Hamilton Naki had better technical skills than I did," Barnard said. "He was a better craftsman than me, especially when it came to stitching, and had very good hands.... His work made my work possible."

When Naki retired in 1991, it was estimated that he had helped more than three thousand medical students hone their skills. He retired quietly on a gardener's pension, and it was only in his last years that his story became known. Before he died, he was awarded an honorary medical degree by the University of Cape Town. His reaction was completely without bitterness. He was proud of what he had done, but the way things had been was just the way things had been. Looking back, he reflected on the covert life he had led. "Nobody was to say what I was doing," he said. "A black person was not supposed to be doing such things. That was the law of the land." But there was relief, as well, in the public recognition. After receiving the Order of Mapungubwe, one of South Africa's highest awards, he said, "I can be happy now that everything is out. The light is lit and the darkness has gone."

And that was Hamilton Naki. So constrained on the outside, so liberated on the inside. What a waste those external constraints were, and how many other Hamilton Nakis have been lost to the world by such discrimination. But what a treasure that internal liberation was, and what an inspiration to so many others.

The reason I particularly wanted to tell Mr. Naki's story today is that something quite remarkable has happened recently here at Elmhurst. Today, in fact, hundreds of Hamilton Nakis have arrived on our campus. Nothing quite so dramatic has happened since about a year ago. These Hamilton Nakis come in various forms—new first-year students, new transfers from other institutions, and new ELSA students, members of our brand-new

Elmhurst Life Skills Academy.

Each of you, of course, has resources to draw on that the original Hamilton Naki could only have dreamed about. More importantly, each of you has the freedom to grow, to stretch, and to explore options. But the most valuable thing you have that makes you a modern-day Hamilton Naki is a spark—a bit of light deep inside. As you discover your passion, as you find that thing that so excites you that you begin stealing with your eyes and using the opportunities you have, you could make that light glow with your unique brilliance.

What do you think that other Hamilton Naki would say to you as you begin your Elmhurst College years? Perhaps it would be as simple as asking you to remember an old song. Some of you will recall it from summer camp. For some of us it will forever be associated with the Civil Rights Movement, when people joined hands and sang it—along with others, like "We Shall Overcome." It is a humble spiritual that on the surface is almost childlike, but which packs the most powerful promise you could make to yourself right now:

> *This little light of mine*
> *I'm gonna let it shine;*
> *Let it shine, let it shine, let it shine.*

I know that's a pretty big assignment to start out with, but there's more. And it has to do with all those other Hamilton Nakis in this room. You have come to join a college, not to sit alone in a corner. And that is because the other people here will push you and encourage you and irritate you and embrace you and make you think again and help you toward your goal. And you must agree to do the same for them. It should go without saying that you must never be a party to the sort of discrimination that your namesake faced. But it goes beyond that. So let's have a second verse that speaks to the responsibility you are assuming—you and the faculty and all of us—for your new colleagues. By joining our college, this is what you are promising to each other:

That little light of yours
I'm gonna help it shine;
Help it shine, help it shine, help it shine.

You are here to nurture that small spark within you, and you are here because others can help you do that, and you can in turn help them nurture the spark inside them.

And I am not quite finished. A fine college is not just a place for private benefit. It is a living and growing organism that we strengthen and improve as we exercise it. Lots of people have labored and sacrificed to create this special, beautiful place called Elmhurst College. There is a spark of greatness here. So I hope each of you will come to understand why the third verse of our little song is so important to us and to the generations of students who will be sitting where you are now long after you are out in the world shining brightly. It is about this school we love, Elmhurst, and the pride we feel in what we are building here:

This little light of ours
We're gonna make us shine;
Make us shine, make us shine, make us shine.

So welcome to you, Hamilton Naki, in all your various shapes and sizes. With high confidence that together we can become a true company of scholars, what college ought to be, I officially convene the 135th academic year of Elmhurst College. The year ahead has every promise of being a truly wonderful one.

   Let it shine, let it shine, let it shine!

ELEVEN

Strengthening the Foundation

THE PRESIDENT'S BREAKFAST FOR
COMMUNITY LEADERS
MARCH 4, 2006

Winchester is a quiet town southwest of London that is about the size of Elmhurst, but a great deal older. Its High Street, dating from Roman times, is thought to be the oldest city street in England. Alfred the Great made Winchester the center of his kingdom and was buried there in 899 in what was already an ancient Saxon church. When William the Conqueror left the field of battle at Hastings in 1066 to claim the crown of England, he established Winchester and London as joint capital cities. Soon thereafter, William installed his cousin as bishop at Winchester, and work was begun on replacing the old minster with a new cathedral in the Norman style.

What we know as Winchester Cathedral was created over the next four centuries as this magnificent structure with the longest nave in Medieval Europe was built and rebuilt and adapted to changing styles. The brutal King William Rufus was buried there in 1100. It was the scene of the marriage of Mary Tudor and Philip of Spain in 1554. The tomb of Izaak Walton, the "compleat angler," is in a part of the south transept known as Fishermen's Chapel. Jane Austen was buried under the north aisle in 1817. For almost a thousand years, Winchester Cathedral has stood and watched a lot of history, and in the 1960s, according to the New Vaudeville Band's hit song, it even stood and watched as "my baby left town."

But in the early years of the last century, disaster loomed for this great treasure. By 1905, huge cracks had appeared in the south wall, and the consulting engineers soon concluded that the problem lay deep underground. The simple fact—which had been lying in wait for hundreds of years—was that the cathedral had been built not on solid ground, but on a peat bog. The original architects, not able to reach bedrock because of the high water table, laid layers of huge beech logs on the damp peat and built the great stone walls on top, in effect floating the cathedral on a raft in the soggy ground.

And it had worked—at least, for quite a few centuries. But eventually the peat layer began to compress with the enormous weight, undermining the foundation and threatening to break the back of the cathedral. There was a real danger that the whole building would simply collapse. As teams of masons set to work regrouting the walls and installing reinforcing rods, the lead engineer became convinced that nothing would really help until the foundation was secure. Somehow they would have to get underneath the walls, deep below the water table, and replace the rotting timbers with firm footings.

And thus began—exactly one hundred years ago this month— the remarkable story of William Walker. Walker was an experienced deep-sea diver, able to use the crude equipment of his day to work on harbor maintenance and underwater salvage jobs. But what he did underneath Winchester Cathedral was truly extraordinary. Each day he would don his two hundred pounds of gear and have his diving helmet bolted down, and he would ease himself down a hole bored next to the wall, down underwater below the lowest stones. There he gradually cleared away the rotting timbers and the peat and began to build up a new base from the underlying hard gravel twenty to twenty-two feet below the surface. The work was grueling—six hours a day under water, often in a prone position, in murky darkness that no artificial light could penetrate, working alone because there wasn't room for any helpers, feeling his way along under a massive building and under the graves of centuries.

The job took five and one-half years. In all, 235 holes were dug around the cathedral to give Walker access to his underwater work site. It is estimated that it took nearly 28,000 bags of concrete, 115,000 concrete blocks, and 900,000 bricks to build a secure underpinning between the solid layer below the peat and the bottom of the cathedral's foundation. The high water table remained, and the crypt of the cathedral is still typically flooded much of the year. But because of William Walker, the foundation is firm. Or, as one writer has put it, "The Conqueror's cousin set the cathedral on a bog. William Walker set it on a rock."

Walker died in the flu epidemic of 1918, but his work is well remembered at Winchester Cathedral. A statue of him in his diving gear is inscribed to "William Walker, who saved the cathedral with his own hands."

But William Walker left behind more than just bricks and mortar. That striking image of a courageous diver struggling in the dark to build new underpinnings beneath a great cathedral holds a message for us today—for us in our time, for us in a dangerous and uncertain world, for us in our very own city of Elmhurst. It is a reminder that sometimes there is just no substitute for going deep down below the surface and strengthening the foundation.

So much of our daily lives is taken up with the busyness of work and home and acquiring and entertainment that it's hard to find the moments when we can step back and think about the foundations of our lives and of our communities. Let me suggest three things that we might want to think about when we do have those rare moments. As it happens, they are all *E*-words. Those who know the history of this 135-year-old college will recognize this device as something that goes back into our past. This college was originally created to provide pastors for the churches being founded by German settlers. The idea was to send the young men on to the Church's seminary in St. Louis, then as now called Eden Seminary, and then on to the ministry. For a very long time this pattern was referred to throughout the denomination as the "triple E"—Elmhurst, Eden, Eternity—and there are still students who take that route. So in the Elmhurst tradition of the "triple E," here are three more *E*s that are important to us—three things for us to think about as we bolt down our helmets and dive down to check out the foundations.

Let's start with *ethics*. I don't need to go through the litany of examples of the scandals that fill the daily news, but it does seem as though we live in an ethically challenged era. Nevertheless, most of us still recognize the need to hold onto our concepts of right and wrong and apply them in our lives as family members, as business decision makers, or as civic leaders. We know it can make a difference when we ask the simple questions—is this honest, is this in line with the rules I have been taught or those I wish others would follow? And we know we can make a difference when we support efforts to hold up some basic rules as reminders to ourselves and others—programs like Character Counts here in Elmhurst, for example.

But what might it mean to dive deeper? One way to think of ethics is to see it not as a set of rules but as a discipline of thought. In this sense, a commitment to ethics means thinking deeply about the moral choices we make and the principles and patterns behind those choices. Ethics is not only about testing our behavior against a set of simple rules. It is also about testing our principles and practices and tracing them down to where they rest—or don't rest—on solid ground.

Take any issue of what we might call applied ethics; that is, the hot-button questions on which reasonable people differ, but that the media want us to see as black and white—or at least red and blue. How easy it is to stand on the surface and throw ethical bricks around. I am ethical because I take this position; you must therefore be unethical because you would vote differently. The issues at hand are too important, and the process of ethical thinking is too valuable, to risk being diminished in this way.

A real commitment to ethics invites you to suit up and accompany William Walker down to where the questions are hard but the connections may be mushy. Are my views on particular issues firmly attached to underlying principles that I can explain to my satisfaction? Or have I simply adopted a platform of someone else's creation? Are the underlying principles I lean on still relevant? As the fine old hymn says, "New occasions teach new duties; Time makes ancient good uncouth." Have my deepest convictions caught up with my deepest thinking? And perhaps most challenging, has self-righteousness seeped into the crevasses, so that cracks have begun to appear; for example, have I become proud of my humility? I will never forget the flash of insight I experienced one day in elementary school when our teacher told the class, "You should never boast; I never boast." When we are struggling with ethical dilemmas down at the foundations, we are closer to the bedrock of true integrity.

So a commitment to ethics pulls us into serious thinking. But our shared humanity calls on us to temper such rigorous analysis with a second *E—empathy*. Human relationships have always been about getting out of our own shell and connecting with another, coming to understand a bit of how that person understands the world and how he or she feels about it. This seems to come naturally when people get to know one another well, and if we still lived, as our distant ancestors did, in small isolated villages, the circle of our empathy might embrace our whole communities. But our world is different. We may argue about how we should manage the globalization of our daily life, but we know there is no turning back. We may not yet be true citizens of an interdependent world, but we are surely residents. How are we supposed to develop empathy toward people we barely know or have no way of knowing at all, people with whom we don't have much in common, even people who seem to us to have no particular interest in developing empathy themselves?

And yet, empathy is foundational. Healthy communities are invariably built on it. Empathy is the essential key that unlocks the problem of dealing with differences—arguably the fundamental challenge of our time on both local and global levels. Once again, when we stand on the surface, empathy may not seem much of a challenge—until we see the cracks. It's easy to assume that all we have to do is treat each other equally, and by the way there's no racism here. But in the dark recesses under the foundation, as we work to really understand another person or another group or those people over there, we come to realize that the long, patient process of building connections—one brick at a time—takes a lot longer, is a lot harder, and is ultimately so much more rewarding. A real commitment to empathy—to sincere understanding and deep concern for all of God's children—is not something to be undertaken lightly, but those who are willing to dive into those waters are the heroes of our time.

Finally, we come to one more *E*, and it is *education*, the *E* that is the big idea behind the college you are visiting this morning. If we want to live as ethical and empathetic people, and if we want to live in ethical and empathetic communities, we need to give some serious attention to how we get there and how we plan to sustain those values over time. While it is tempting to speak primarily about the education that takes place in this particular private college, I want to focus on the general responsibilities we all share for the education of the next generation of our community, of our nation, and of the world. Perhaps because there are so many different educational institutions embedded in a complex organizational web, we may sometimes need to remind ourselves and our communities of our basic, shared, public responsibilities as citizens. As is often the case, we find in the words of Abraham Lincoln a model of clear and forceful thinking. In his very first political announcement in March of 1832 he wrote: "Upon the subject of education…I can only say that I view it as the most important subject which we as a people can be engaged in."

That cuts through a lot, doesn't it? "The most important subject we as a people can be engaged in." What would it mean to take that assertion seriously? What would it mean for our public-policy priorities? What would it mean for the value we place on the work of teachers? What would it mean for our tax rates? What would it mean for how we vote on local school referenda? "The most important subject we as a people can be engaged in." Lincoln puts the education of our children right down there at the foundation. And until we have put every bag of concrete and every brick we can find down there where it will count the most, we have not done everything we can do keep the walls above solid through the years.

So I leave you with three big *E*s to ponder as you leave Elmhurst College—EC, if you will—and go out into the world that calls you. Ethics, empathy, and education are at the foundation of our lives together and of the communities in which we live. They are commitments we take seriously here at your college, and we know from your friendship and support that you take them seriously as well. William Walker's diving helmet reminds us that if we are willing to be courageous, we can indeed work on those foundations and make them stronger. And the great cathedral that stands now on firm footings is a testimony to the difference individuals can make. William Walker's memorial at Winchester says he "saved the cathedral with his own hands." What will we save with ours?

TWELVE

Mentor's College

THE PRESIDENT'S BREAKFAST FOR
COMMUNITY LEADERS
MARCH 3, 2007

I t is a pleasure to welcome you all to Elmhurst College. This is the thirteenth time I have attended this breakfast, and I must say I still can't quite figure it out. Why nearly three hundred community leaders and friends of the College would come out at 7:30 on a Saturday morning in March is something of a mystery to me. A couple of weeks ago I was telling the president of another college about this upcoming event, and he agreed it was pretty unusual. "Well," he said, "they must really care about the College." And if that's at least part of what's behind this mystery, then we at Elmhurst College are very grateful.

I'm pleased to report that the college you care about is strong and healthy, and the students here are learning and growing. The number of applicants for spots in our freshman class is more than twice what it was a decade ago, and the test scores of the students we accept are on average 20 percent higher. The graduation rate has gone up from about the national average to a level that *U.S. News & World Report* has recognized as one of the highest among our kind of college. Very importantly, the campus is a much more active and vibrant place than ever before, in part because more students are choosing to live on campus. And we're taking a big step in the direction of an even stronger College with the construction of a new residence hall.

The physical campus is the most visible indicator of change, and that new residence hall and the adjacent parking areas are the first steps in the implementation of an important long-term campus master plan the College has been working on. Today we roll out the official report of that planning process. The brochure in front of you came off the press just a few days ago, and it's particularly appropriate to share the very first copies with the community leaders in this room, many of whom contributed to the process. As you will see, the plan describes how the current footprint of the campus might be built out over the coming decades in a way that makes it an even greater community resource, with a multilevel deck to concentrate parking, a performing arts center for the community to share, enlarged athletic facilities, and a commitment to green architecture and design that will give new meaning to our arboretum tradition. So take it with you, study it at your leisure, and join with us in dreaming about what this corner of our city might become in the years ahead.

But you in this room this morning know very well that institutions are much more than bricks and mortar. It's great to have a beautiful and well-maintained space in which to live and work, but the more important question is what goes on *within* that space. I want to think with you this morning about some of the principles by which we build good colleges and good communities in which people learn and grow.

To do so, I'm going to reach back past the numbers of today, past the plans of the moment, to one of the great early touchstones of Western civilization. Specifically, I want to turn to Homer, the Greek poet who lived in the eighth century B.C. We have no idea who Homer really was, but the two great epic poems attached to his name, *The Iliad* and *The Odyssey,* have resonated through the ages. The stories have been told and retold, and the themes and characters are fixtures in our common heritage. For example, if you have read *Cold Mountain*, the novel by Charles Frazier, or if you have seen the film *O Brother Where Art Thou*, then you know the basic story line of *The Odyssey*.

As we read in *The Iliad*, the Greek king Odysseus doesn't really want to leave home and risk his life to conquer the city of Troy, but he finally follows his destiny, says good-bye to his family, and joins the great struggle. The fighting is fierce, and full of twists and turns, such as the brilliant trick of hiding Greek soldiers inside a great wooden horse presented to the Trojans as a gift. Odysseus earns a reputation as a strong leader, known for his shrewdness and courage. Many heroic men and women perish in the long conflict, but the Greeks eventually prevail, and Odysseus sets out to return home.

The Odyssey tells of the return of Odysseus to his kingdom and his family on the island of Ithaca, a very long journey of many wanderings and adventures. He and his men have to fight their way out of all sorts of complicated jams. He battles the one-eyed giant Cyclops and is captured by the sea nymph Calypso. He survives the temptations of the Sirens and the storms sent by the angry god Poseidon. Along the way he meets fascinating people and hears wonderful stories. Meanwhile, back at home, his faithful wife, Penelope, waits for Odysseus as the years go by—it would eventually be twenty-two years.

But there is another figure in this tale. Odysseus also left behind his young son, Telemachus, born just before Odysseus set sail for Troy. One of the subplots in the epic tells how the boy develops from a shy and awkward youth into a competent and courageous young man during the decades of his father's absence. Telemachus, too, has many learning experiences along the way. But he does not have them by accident.

Before he left home, Odysseus asked his most trustworthy

friend to look after his household, and especially his young son. His friend made a solemn promise to Odysseus that he would be there for Telemachus whatever happened. That old and trusted friend's name was Mentor. Mentor was a man of integrity who devoted himself to fulfilling his promise to Odysseus. But there is a fascinating twist to the story. Because this is, after all, Greek mythology, the gods get involved.

Athena, the most important goddess, is traditionally associated with wisdom, but she is far from an aloof or ivory-tower thinker. She is known for getting around with lightning speed and for always being where the action is. She often appears in Greek art wearing a helmet pushed up on her forehead, but ready to be pulled down to cover her face when necessary. Athena is the goddess of wisdom, but it is a wisdom that is always ready to engage the real world, to fight if necessary, sometimes even in disguise, if that will get the job done. When Athena wants to get a message to young Telemachus, she adopts a disguise and assumes the shape and voice of Mentor. So Mentor always ends up saying just the right thing and giving Telemachus just the help he needs because, when it matters most, Athena is speaking through him.

Here, for example, is the exchange when Telemachus travels to Pylos to ask the powerful Prince Nestor for news of his long-lost father. Homer records it this way: Mentor (actually Athena in disguise) accompanies him on the voyage to provide encouragement, and just before their meeting with the great Nestor, he (she?) nudges the young man along and tells him not to be shy. But Telemachus, very unsure of himself, asks for advice. "Mentor," he says, "how am I to go up to such a great man? How shall I greet him? Remember that I have had no practice in making speeches, and a young man may well hesitate to cross-examine one so much his senior." Mentor (at least the young man thinks it's Mentor) answers this way: "Telemachus, your native wit will serve you well, and when that fails, heaven will inspire you. The gods have watched your progress ever since your birth. Do you think they will stop now?" In other words, show some self-confidence, you have a lot going for you, and I'll be here when you need me.

And so we have, in one of the oldest written stories in human history, the model for all mentors since then. The key elements repeat themselves every time this unique relationship is established. A young person, bright, respectful, and energetic, but with little experience. An older person, willing to pay attention and to give good advice. And it turns out, when the mentor is performing this role well, he or she has, probably without knowing it, a spark of the divine, so that the mentor is even more helpful than he or she realizes.

Well, Odysseus finally makes it back home, only to discover his wife besieged by suitors who have been trying for years—unsuccessfully—to make her forget her absent husband. There is a climactic and brutal battle, in which Odysseus, joined by his now quite grown-up son, Telemachus, handily defeats all the suitors, and Odysseus and Penelope presumably live happily ever after.

But let us not say good-bye to Professor Mentor too hastily. Yes, it's a charming story that explains how what we call mentoring got its name. But perhaps there is something more for us in that ancient story. We're here today to celebrate a special college and to recognize the special community that is its home. What might Mentor (or perhaps Mentor with Athena's inspiration) have to contribute to our understanding of how to build a good college and a good community? If Mentor were to visit Elmhurst, what might he have to say?

The first guiding principle of Mentor's College might well be: Keep the promise. One of the most immediately striking things about Mentor is his absolute integrity—in spite of all the lying and treachery that is an almost constant undercurrent in *The Odyssey*. He has made a promise to his friend, and he keeps it. Think of all the ways this commitment to keeping promises is at the core of good teaching—and good learning. We commit ourselves to our students. We commit ourselves to pursuing our disciplines with honesty and thoroughness. We commit ourselves to evaluation that is careful and fair. We expect students to commit themselves to honest effort and active participation. And on and on. Our integrity as scholars, and teachers, and people comes first. At Mentor's College it would always be clear that promises are to be kept.

Next, I think Mentor would want us to observe that he spent years helping Telemachus grow as a whole person. When Odysseus was at last reunited with his son, he was delighted to find a young man with considerable technical skills—he knew how to use a sword very well. But much more important was his son's character—his courage, his loyalty, his faithfulness. A good college needs to teach so much more than literature and biology and accounting, as critical as those are. The learning that goes on in sports and campus activities, in international travel and internships, and most of all in interaction with people of character—all this leads to whole people who are committed and balanced and courageous. Mentor's College would be a school for character as well as competence.

A third principle of Mentor's College emerges from that special relationship with Athena. To succeed in getting our message through, we must put a human face on what we want to teach and speak with a human voice. To speak with a human voice is to interact directly as people. It is to take the time to get to know each other, to listen carefully to each other, to share ourselves with others. Athena would remind us that if we want to help young people grow, we must give ourselves to them as people, we must enter their daily lives as mentors. This is why I am pretty convinced that if Mentor himself were designing an institution of higher learning, it would be a small college. The large public and private universities that so many students attend have some attractive features, but a good small college can really shine when it comes to mentoring.

One more principle. Some of us have learned the phrase "watchful waiting" through the tragic experience of monitoring cancer. The associations may be painful, but it is a compelling expression nonetheless. I think Mentor would urge us to build into our college the willingness to watch and wait. This is a special discipline that is perhaps more active and intentional than it might at first seem. Just waiting, by itself, can be passive and likely to drift into indifference. Watchful waiting means careful attention and concern combined with patience and freedom. "The gods have watched your progress since your birth," says Mentor, and Telemachus steps forward with confidence. I have spent a fair amount of time over the years meeting with Elmhurst alumni, and I have been impressed by how often the stories they tell involve someone noticing them, someone realizing when they needed a word of encouragement or challenge, someone simply paying attention. One of the miracles of human interaction is how much we can strengthen others by simply paying attention, by watchful waiting.

So there you have four principles—four standards by which we might tell if a college might fairly be called Mentor's College:

Keep the promise.
Build the whole person.

Speak with a human voice.
Wait and watch.

These are exactly the challenges that good colleges like Elmhurst strive to live up to every day. And might not Mentor's messages to the good college serve the good community as well? A good community is, after all, a garden for growing people. So let's begin with keeping the promise. If we say we have good schools, let's make darn sure they really are; that they have the resources and the community-wide commitment to excellence that our young people deserve. Then, let's concentrate on building whole people. Let's be sure that culture and recreation and spiritual life are valued and supported. Mentor and Athena would both smile, I think, when a really good public library and a fine art museum and a busy park district and an active Y and a great college and engaged churches, forward-looking local business leaders, and the professionals who provide public services are all seeking ways to help each other and especially to show our young people by example that "character counts."

In the good community, people will seek out ways to put a human face on their responsibilities to each other, to help out in organizations in person, to visit those who have no visitors, to be there when our neighbors need a hand, and to serve as real mentors ourselves whenever we have the chance. And finally, the good community pays attention. In the spirit of watchful waiting, true community leaders observe how life is actually playing out for people. They find the good and praise it, they try to notice when things are not what they should be, they seek out partners for projects that will make things better, they reach out to people who are different and let them know they are important too, they encourage freedom and fresh ideas.

In our time, the name of Mentor has come to stand for a person who has made a commitment to be there for someone who wants to grow. The story of the original Mentor fleshes out the concept and reminds us of how important it is to create whole institutions and communities of Mentors. The story itself is a very old one, crafted by ancient people we can never hope to fully understand, passed on at first by an oral tradition and finally copied down almost three millennia ago at the dawn of the written word. But it is a story that has never stopped being created. Every day at Elmhurst College and in the community of Elmhurst, modern Mentors step forward to nurture the next generation and to share their inspiration with others who will themselves pass on this essential part of our human heritage to the Mentors of the future.

And lest anyone leave today thinking that Mentor was just a nice old man who helped a young person but who wasn't relevant to the big issues that public leaders have to deal with, let Homer have the last word. At the very end of this immense saga—one thousand pages in modern print—the venerable Mentor (really Athena in her best disguise) steps right into the middle of the biggest issue of his day. Our heroes are stuck in a savage battle they don't know how to stop. Telemachus has proven his courage, Odysseus and his family are reunited, and the enemies of Ithaca have been defeated. But the violence has developed a life of its own, and Athena has one more job to do. Odysseus and his colleagues, of course, will see only Mentor. Here are the final lines of *The Odyssey*:

Odysseus and his gallant son charged straight at the front lines,
Slashing away with swords, with two-edged spears and now
They would have killed them all, cut them off from home

if Athena, daughter of storming Zeus, had not cried out
in a piercing voice that stopped all fighters cold,
"Hold back, you men of Ithaca, back from brutal war!
Break off—shed no more blood—make peace at once!"
. . . . .
So she commanded. He obeyed her, glad of heart.
And Athena handed down her pacts of peace
Between both sides for all the years to come—
the daughter of Zeus whose shield is storm and thunder,
yes, but the goddess still kept Mentor's [form] and voice.

So Homer's final image is of Mentor—divinely inspired Mentor—in the thick of things, still guiding, still teaching, and thereby making a better world. It is an image I invite you to take with you as you return to all the opportunities you have to guide and teach and thereby make a better world. Thank you for coming to college this morning. Thank you for your commitment to this great school and this great community, and for all you do to keep Mentor's form and voice alive in Elmhurst.

IV *Our Heritage*

THIRTEEN

The Isiness of Was

THE 125TH ANNIVERSARY GALA
DECEMBER 6, 1996

We live in an era that is focused on *is*. The question most people ask most of the time—when they bother to look outside themselves at all—is "What's happening?"—what is going on *today*. *Is* is what we find when we look with eyes that see only today. But to focus only on *is* is to see with only one weak eye. Such seeing lacks depth perception, peripheral vision, and perspective. When we see only *is*, we have the illusion that we are seeing the real thing, living in "the real world." How sadly mistaken we are, when we limit ourselves to living only in the world of *is*.

Many branches of learning teach a very different truth. When we study mathematical statistics we come to understand very quickly that a single number, by itself, tells us nothing; a number has meaning only if it is placed in the context of other numbers, so that we can make a comparison or describe a trend. Modern physical science constantly reminds us of the reality and critical importance of the dimension of time. And the study of psychology and human behavior makes clear that we cannot begin to understand an individual without some knowledge of his or her past experience. We know very little if all we know is *is*. *Is* gains meaning only in the context of *was*, and *was* is very much a part of *is*. So my remarks on this special anniversary occasion are essentially about the "*isiness*" of *was*. Or, to put all I have to say in the simplest possible terms, *was is*.

And what a wonderful opportunity we have had in this year-long celebration of Elmhurst College's 125th birthday to grasp this reality—the *isiness* of *was*—in a fresh and vivid way. From the fine book on our history, to the banners around the campus, to the rediscovery of the Hash Bell and the syrup pot, to the reenactment of the arrival of Inspektor Kranz and his fourteen young students at the Elmhurst railroad station, to the birthday celebration on campus earlier today, to this festive evening, we have caught many glimpses of the *was* that is so much a part of our *is*.

So this anniversary has been so much more than a mere excuse for a party. Of course, we've had fun, but underneath the surface, a true learning experience has been going on. We have been taking lessons in the *isiness* of *was*. And out of this experience has come a renewed sense of what is important about the reality of Elmhurst College and what a difference *was* makes.

It makes a difference that Elmhurst began its life in the year 1871. That was a remarkable moment in the history of our country and of higher education. So many things happened in 1871, or just a year or two before or after, so many things that are part of who we are today. It was a period of national expansiveness in which the United States bought Alaska and completed the Transcontinental Railroad, and finally, six years after the Civil War, declared legal amnesty for the citizens of the South. It was a period of change in which women first won the right to vote—even though it was only within the Territory of Wyoming. And it was a time in which some young men from Princeton and Rutgers got together for the first intercollegiate contest in a game they called football. It was also a time of crises faced and overcome, from the great Chicago Fire, less than two months before the founding of Elmhurst College, to the disastrous bank failures and depression that began when our school was less than two years old.

The time right around 1871 was a time of daring new ventures in colleges and universities, innovations that changed the face of higher education as we know it today. The spread of colleges into the country west of the Atlantic seaboard gave us Syracuse and Purdue and Lewis & Clark and Vanderbilt and St. Olaf. The rise of the land-grant college gave us Cornell and Ohio State and Oregon State. A new interest in education for women gave us Wellesley and Smith. An awareness of the need to provide opportunities for newly liberated African Americans gave us Howard and Morehouse and Tougaloo. New efforts in Catholic education gave us Loyola and St. John's and St. Peter's; interest in technical education gave us Stevens Institute and Virginia Polytechnic and Rose-Hulman. And remember, all this was within a year or two of the founding of Elmhurst College.

And more than the opening of new institutions was involved in this exciting time. Back in Massachusetts, President Eliot was introducing a new curriculum at staid old Harvard, something known as the elective system, where students could choose from among a range of courses, and the first official course in music was offered as an elective in 1871. That same year, Eliot pushed the boundaries even further and proposed that daily chapel services at Harvard be made voluntary instead of mandatory, and that radical step would have taken place if it had not been for the strong opposition of a member of the Board of Overseers by the name of Ralph Waldo Emerson.

In that vibrant and exciting year, certainly unheralded at the time, young Carl Kranz got off the train at the Elmhurst station, herded together his tired flock of fourteen students, and went looking for their baggage. You know the rest of the story—how the baggage car was lost, with all their belongings and books and everything they needed to start a school, and how they managed anyway, with a little help from their new friends in the community.

As a college president, I must say that that image has a certain uncomfortably contemporary feel about it—the image of Inspektor Kranz standing there, no doubt feeling very responsible for the young people in his charge, full of great hopes and dreams about the school yet to be, but stranded without the resources even to change his socks.

But there were more important realities in our past that have shaped our present. Our Germanic heritage is something you really have to understand about Elmhurst. For more than a third of our history, the language of instruction was German—for a while even English was taught in German. The names of our campus buildings reflect that heritage, as do the names of our presidents (at least until this Welshman showed up!). And perhaps the College's long tradition of meticulous maintenance and a certain—shall we say—carefulness about rules and procedures reflects a deeply rooted cultural style, one way in which *was is*.

I believe an even more powerful continuity in Elmhurst's history has been what we now often refer to on campus as "purposeful learning." This has always been a school that has nurtured a sense of vocation in its students, and from the early days of preparing young men for the ministry, liberal arts education and preparation for professional life have always been seen as complementing one another. And as the circle was widened to include students preparing for other careers, students from outside the denomination, then women and commuters, then older students, and then students from a variety of racial and ethnic backgrounds—through all the enlargements of its mission, one constant was that the College continued to take very seriously what kind of person the student was becoming and what kind of contribution the graduate would be prepared to make in his or her life's work. And that is exactly where we are today.

Here is one more example of the stamp of history on today—the *isiness* of *was*. This one brings us back to Inspektor Kranz, not so much at that moment of truth on the railroad platform but rather what he did on December 7th—and 8th and 9th. In spite of all the facts to the contrary, he simply set to work fulfilling his dreams, and by early January he had classes under way. It was a pattern repeated again and again. Perhaps the most pointed illustration in our history is the scene of President Dinkmeyer in 1948, without the means to pay for a desperately needed building, having a big hole dug anyway and putting up a sign declaring, "A Hole To Be Filled With Faith." He did that three times in his presidency, and those holes *were* filled and became Lehmann Hall, Dinkmeyer Hall, and Hammerschmidt Chapel. "A Hole To Be Filled By Faith." That's the way Elmhurst College has survived and flourished over 125 years. People have taken dreams that seemed impossible and dug in and made them real.

This is our heritage too; this is our *was* that *is*. And I think this brings us to a way of looking toward the future as well as toward the past. For just as on this anniversary we celebrate the *isiness* of *was*, so we need to remind ourselves of the *isiness* of *will be*. The college Elmhurst will become is being forged on the anvil of today. We will best honor our heritage as a college by digging some holes ourselves, by imagining the best possible future for this school we love and for the students we serve—and then getting past the missing baggage and all the limitations that will inevitably get in our way, and working with faith and determination to make it happen.

My thanks to each of you in this room for all you have done and all you are doing—and yes, all you will do—to make this era in our history one we can be proud of when we pass Elmhurst College on to those who will follow. Thank you, and Happy Birthday Elmhurst!

Etched in Stone

THE PRESIDENT'S HOLIDAY DINNER
DECEMBER 7, 2003

There are times when we just don't want to make commitments. Perhaps we have floated an idea at a committee meeting or in a family discussion, but we don't really want people to take it *too* seriously. Or we may be negotiating a deal or a price, or arguing a point, but we want the other side to understand we're flexible. In all such cases, a handy cliché awaits to keep things up in the air: "It's not etched in stone."

Sometimes it seems that much of life, in fact, is not etched in stone, but rather scribbled in sand. We come to expect that the words of today will be washed away by tomorrow. So when we do come across something that actually *is* etched in stone, we have an irresistible urge to read the words and, if possible, run our fingers over the letters and feel their sharp edges and their permanence. This summer a local newspaper ran a photograph of a stonecutter up on a lift carving the name "A. C. Buehler Library" above the new entrance of Elmhurst College's latest renovation, and the message was clear—this is an important place; remember this name.

That photograph got me thinking about the things that are etched in stone around the campus. There are other building names, of course—we pass under the boldly inscribed words "Hammerschmidt Memorial Chapel" each time we enter for a service or lecture or concert. But what other things have, over the years, seemed important enough to chisel into walls? Might there be, in the words the College tries to help us remember, some insights into the soul of this school we love? Might we find, in Shakespeare's phrase, "sermons in stones"?

Come with me, then, for a little tour of the campus that our college shares with the Elmhurst community. We'll make five quick stops at places where there are carved words from which to learn.

A good place to begin is where so much of the College began, the oldest campus building, known today as Old Main. When the *Hauptgebaüde*, or Main Building, was put up in 1878 for the impressive price of $25,000, it was a sign that the little fledgling school really did have a future. High above the doorway, the builders chiseled the formal name of what was then only informally called Elmhurst College. And more than just a name; it was a statement of mission and purpose. I will spare you any attempt to recite the text in German, but in translation it proclaims: "Pre-seminary of the German Evangelical Synod of North America."

Many of you know the rest of the story that makes these words etched in stone an especially poignant part of the Elmhurst saga. Sometime in the late 1940s, just after the end of the Second World War, a mason climbed a ladder with a bucket of cement and covered over the lettering, leaving a smooth, blank surface. In the space, a large metal casting of the College seal was installed, and the old German inscription faded from memory.

The best guess is that this unusual attempt to obscure what a prior generation had etched in stone reflected a concern that the returning veterans flocking to the campus might not appreciate the very German inscription. Perhaps the leaders at the time wanted to put aside the early experience of the institution and draw attention instead to the college of their time. But however it happened, it was one step—perhaps a false one—in the long road from the College's beginnings as a small, insular school for German-speaking boys preparing to preach in German-American churches to its current role as a leading liberal arts college serving a diverse and multifaceted student body.

Some of you here remember the renovation of Old Main in the mid-1980s when workmen sandblasting the exterior discovered the bit of history that had been all but forgotten. Now that those carved words have been uncovered and restored, they serve as a daily reminder of the deep roots of the College and of those strong, devout people—those strangers in a strange land—who contributed so much to the special character of Elmhurst and of America.

The next time you walk by those words etched in stone, stop and reflect a moment on the complex layers of history there and the reminder of the risks of allowing the passions of the day to wipe out what is special about our heritage.

Come now across campus to see the next message, this one carved over the entrance to the College's first gymnasium, the building we now know as Goebel Hall. Many Elmhurst alumni played basketball there before it was transformed into a home for administrative offices that directly serve students. When the building was designed in the mid-1920s, it represented a big leap in Elmhurst's efforts to become a real, fully equipped college. But the creators of the modern Elmhurst College were not about to send mixed signals concerning the appropriate role of athletics. So they turned to the classics, specifically to John Milton's seventeenth-century dramatic poem *Samson Agonistes*.

In the text, the mighty Samson, having thoughtlessly betrayed his great gift of physical power, is defeated, blinded, and imprisoned, but still struggling to understand and learn from his devastating experience. Here are his words, as they appear on the old gymnasium: "What is strength without a double share of wisdom? Vast, unwieldy, burdensome."

No ambiguity there for the student athletes who would enter the building. Academics come first! But a broader message remains long after the echoes of bouncing balls have died away. Whatever gifts you have, whatever strengths, must be used with wisdom. You are responsible for bringing thoughtfulness, careful analysis, and good judgment to your choices, and as your gifts increase, your need for wisdom grows exponentially. It is a sermon in stone to remember as we enjoy our blessings as individuals, as a community, and as a superpower on the international stage. "What is strength without a double share of wisdom?"

Stroll back now to the east side of the campus for a pair of quotations from two of Elmhurst's favorite sons. For several years now, Reinhold Niebuhr has been standing there, permanently caught in the moment of saying something very important. You don't need to know anything about the man himself to sense the energy and passion of that professorial stance. But if you do look for words, they are there as well. The little prayer that Niebuhr wrote in the summer of 1943 for a Sunday service in the country church in Heath, Massachusetts, has become one of history's most repeated prayers—and perhaps one of its most misunderstood:

> *God, give us the serenity to accept the things that cannot be changed;*
> *Give us the courage to change the things that should be changed;*
> *Give us the wisdom to distinguish one from the other.*

In a way, it is unfortunate that this has come to be known as the "Serenity Prayer." Reinhold Niebuhr was not one to preach the quiet acceptance of the inevitable. Acting with courage was more his style, but he insisted that courage always be informed by realism. The prayer is in fact a careful balancing of two ideas in tension—a realistic assessment of the world that dispenses with rose-colored glasses and an idealism that goes to work trying to make the world a better place. So, by the grace of God, learn what the world is really like, with all the flaws and limitations you will not be able to overcome, but never let that stop you from fighting injustice and inhumanity and all the other things that should be changed. And, managing the tension in that paradox is our old friend wisdom. Yes, there is a pattern here, and we see again, chiseled in stone, a profound message about the mission of a college of character.

But nowhere on campus is there a clearer declaration of what the College stands for than at our next stop, the front of the Frick Center. Here Reinhold's younger brother Helmut, later known as H. Richard Niebuhr, gets his say. H. Richard's three years as president in the 1920s were critical years that planted a vision of what Elmhurst College might become. The quotation is from an introduction he prepared for the College yearbook in 1925. "The most urgent need of the present generation..." he wrote, "is light and warmth, the light of knowledge and the warmth of high idealism."

Those words were very much on the minds of those who created the symbol that we have come to associate with the College, with the letter *E* in the form of a flame giving both light and warmth. Once again, though, a Niebuhrian tension. The light of knowledge calls for classrooms and textbooks and facts and research, while the warmth of high idealism draws on experiences, the inspiration of human models, purposefulness, and passion. It would be a lot easier to build an education around just one or the other of these approaches. Niebuhr says you must have both—light and warmth must go together. And while he doesn't use the word, it is clear that Niebuhr finds wisdom where light and warmth come together.

The next time you have a chance to visit the front of the campus, rest there a few moments and reflect on the words of two brothers. In both cases, they seem to be easy on the surface, but if you dig in and study them carefully, you will find things with which to wrestle and from which to learn. And you will find there a good deal of what our college is all about.

One more stop on our tour, this time to the newest words in stone. In recent months, we have been watching a new academic building rising on Alexander Boulevard, enclosing a new campus quadrangle, an attractive and inviting outdoor space to welcome visitors and provide a peaceful vista in our daily travels across campus. We have named the center of this space in honor of the College's alumni. Around the decorative fountain you will begin to see small circles appear in the paving bricks as each graduating class leaves its mark in that spot. We decided early on that we wanted to add some words to Alumni Circle, a special message to graduates that would give current students something to think about as well.

The words we chose come from a play by T. S. Eliot. *The Family Reunion*, which Eliot wrote in 1939, tells the story of a young man, haunted by tragedy, returning to his childhood home. As he tries to piece together the bits of his background that will explain his life and release him from the fears that imprison him, his wise Aunt Agatha cautions him about assumptions made too early and encourages him in his quest. "There is more to understand," she tells him. "Hold fast to that as the way to freedom."

And that, we decided, is the challenge we want to put before our alumni. There is always more to understand. Education is not something one receives or completes. It is a permanent quest for understanding, a lifelong search for wisdom. And behind the quest is that most human of instincts—curiosity. Curiosity drives inquiry and discovery. It keeps us alive and young. And it is the best inoculation we have against one of the greatest threats to our future—minds that are closed and hearts that are without imagination. The real threat to our freedom comes not from the outside, but from the mental complacency that whispers to us that we know everything we need to know, so we don't need to think anymore, we don't need to learn from others who are different from us, and we don't need to question our own actions. That is the way to shallowness, intolerance, and tyranny. Elmhurst College wants to lead its graduates down a different path.

When the weather is better and you have the opportunity to spend a quiet moment in Alumni Circle, begin on the Library side and read as you walk around the fountain. "There is more to understand: Hold fast to that as the way to freedom."

So our short tour has unearthed five treasures, five inscriptions in stone that help tell the College's story across time and express its mission today. "The German Evangelical Synod," "What is strength without wisdom?" "Serenity, Courage, and Wisdom," "Light and Warmth," "More to understand." On this evening of remembering, these words remind us that the College that has brought us together tonight has deep roots and powerful purposes. But these messages etched in stone do not just sit there quietly. Each of them calls us to respond, to commit ourselves, to act.

There are two particular kinds of response I want to suggest tonight. The first is at a very practical level and all of us in this room know how it works. A private college such as Elmhurst exists only as long as it is supported by its friends. And the quality of its work can rarely exceed the quality of its support. Two years ago at this holiday dinner, I announced the public beginning of the largest campaign in the history of the College, designed to run until December of 2004 with a goal of $40,000,000 toward the many long-term needs of the College. A lot of work had already happened behind the scenes, but at that point we rolled up our sleeves and, inspired by Campaign Chair Al Brinkmeier, we got to work together.

Tonight I am pleased to report that, with twelve months yet to go, we have reached, in gifts and pledges, a total of $40,117,467. This is certainly a time to applaud, but it is by no means a time to slow down. Let us redouble our efforts to assure that when we celebrate the closing of the Vision In Action Campaign one year from now, we will have lifted Elmhurst College beyond our original dreams to new levels of strength and quality.

The second response to those sermons in stone that I would suggest we consider is to learn and grow, just as we expect our students to do. Elmhurst is not just a college to support; it is also a college from which to learn. So here is your assignment to take you into the new year. Let us each find some new way to put T. S. Eliot's call into practice in our own daily lives. There is more to understand, and that quest will help us escape the prison of closed minds and closed hearts.

So I challenge each of you to pick one thing you really don't understand. Maybe you really don't understand how people who call themselves good, thoughtful Americans can possibly hold some opinion or political position quite different from yours. So set out to understand them better—to listen to them, to read what they read. That doesn't mean agree. In fact, your better understanding might confirm and strengthen your judgment. But seeking an understanding of the different experiences and thinking that lead to different conclusions might well broaden your perspective and put you in a position to open a doorway through a wall of misunderstanding. Perhaps it is people of a different culture or a different religion that you really don't understand. Or whether free trade is good public policy or not. Or whether global warming is a significant threat. Or what might be done about homelessness. Whatever, choose something worthy of your concern and set out on a quest for understanding.

You will be traveling the pathway toward wisdom. And you will be taking with you the gratitude of the college you support and the encouragement of all those who have left behind words for you to remember. In the weeks and months ahead, may you enjoy the richest of holiday seasons, may you continue to grow through the search for new understanding, and may you know the peace of God, which is beyond understanding.

FIFTEEN
A Culture in the Wilderness

THE PRESIDENT'S HOLIDAY DINNER
DECEMBER 3, 2006

O ne hundred and thirty-five years ago tonight, a young teacher and his small class of boys were completing their preparations for a trip. The story of their arrival and its aftermath is familiar to most of us in this room, but before they stepped off the train, there was the trip itself and all it represented. For most of the little group it would seem just a short journey compared with the long ocean voyage and the crossing of a third of a continent that had taken them from their native Germany to the prairies of Indiana. They knew a bit about their destination. They knew there would be other German settlers there, and they were no doubt encouraged to learn that the town had just adopted a new, German-sounding name. They may not have been aware, until they arrived, that this tiny village of Elmhurst was also crowded with immigrants of another sort, refugees from the Great Fire that had devastated Chicago just a few weeks earlier.

The Reverend Kranz and his fourteen pupils were also probably not consciously thinking that, by taking this journey westward to start a new school in a strange village, they were reenacting—albeit on a small scale—a ritual that had been at the heart of higher education in America since its beginning. The tradition goes back to just a few years after the establishment of the first fragile outposts—in Virginia in 1607 and then in Massachusetts thirteen years later—when as quickly as they were able, the settlers planted a college. One of the earliest written records of New England describes the process this way:

> After God had carried us safe to New England, and wee had builded our houses, provided necessaries for our livlihood, rear'd convenient places for God's worship, and setled the Civill Government: One of the next things we longed for, and looked after was to advance Learning and perpetuate it to Posterity.... And as wee were thinking and consulting how to effect this great Work, it pleased God to stir up the heart of one Mr Harvard (a godly Gentleman, and a lover of Learning,...) to give the one half of his Estate...Towards the erecting of a College.

And so some space was carved out of the wilderness to light the lamp of learning. The location they chose was a riverside hamlet that the colonists named, with outrageous ambition, Cambridge. As the settlements spread along the coast, so did the new colleges. And as the European presence pushed further into the wilderness, so did the tradition of placing new colleges at the leading edge of the frontier. When Dartmouth College was opened in the Royal Province of New Hampshire "for the education and instruction of Youth of the Indian Tribes in this Land...and also of English Youth and any others," its official motto expressed the metaphor that was clearly on the minds of its founders: *Vox Clamantis in Deserto*—"A voice crying in the wilderness."

Fifty years ago this fall, I began my own college years at Maryville College in East Tennessee, an institution that emerged from just such impulses. A young Presbyterian pastor named Isaac Anderson had grown up in Virginia and had accompanied his family as they ventured with their wagons and cattle through the mountain passes to new farmland being developed in what was then "the wilderness beyond the mountains." As soon as he could, he started a little seminary known locally as "Mr. Anderson's log college." By the time I arrived, it had evolved into a solid liberal arts institution, but many of my classes were held in a venerable old building called Anderson Hall, which was the direct descendant of the log college.

Historians have for years debated just how the experience of the wilderness and the frontier affected the development of a distinctly American approach to political community and democracy. There is no question that the great migration and expansion across the continent produced a pattern of higher education quite different from the ancient seats of learning in Europe—Oxford, Cambridge, Paris, and the others—that had anchored scholars through the centuries. Here the college was to be a marker of the advance of civilization, a central instrument of the expansion of a nation. Nowhere is this clearer than in the histories of the many colleges created in the Midwest during the nineteenth century. Former Elmhurst President Robert Stanger put it succinctly in his history of the first century of our college. "The aim of the pioneer founders," he wrote, "was to maintain a culture in the wilderness, to provide an educated leadership for the developing communities, and to teach the liberal arts within the context of the Christian faith."

So the urge to establish and sustain a culture in the wilderness is imprinted in the DNA of colleges such as Elmhurst. But is it just a vestigial shadow that is of only historical interest, a genetic adaptation that once served a purpose but is now only a faint memory? I wonder. Perhaps life today is lived more in the wilderness than we are aware. In recent months we who are the successors of the founders of Elmhurst College have been thinking about how to talk about our mission today. A provisional statement that is currently circulating on campus puts it this way: "It is our special mission to prepare each graduate to think deeply, connect broadly, serve usefully, and live faithfully."

Those objectives are stated in straightforward, everyday terms, but they are profoundly countercultural. Any college that truly achieves them will be moving the frontier forward.

In the wilderness of shallow thinking or no thinking at all, we want our students to be researching, analyzing, evaluating, problem solving, discovering, creating, and growing into people who will think deeply.

In the wilderness of narrowness and hatred, we want our students to cross boundaries, reach for broader perspectives, learn from diversity, experience the breadth of a liberal arts education, and become people who will connect broadly.

In the wilderness of self-centeredness and blindness to the needs of others, we want Elmhurst students to learn how to make a difference, to be true professionals in their chosen fields, engaged citizens, experienced in both teamwork and leadership, and ready to go into the world to serve usefully.

And in the wilderness of corruption and evasion of responsibility, we want students at our college to think through and assume personal ownership of their values and then keep faith with them as they hold themselves accountable and live faithfully.

So perhaps it is not that hard to connect the impulses that motivated the creation of our college to the everyday work of the Elmhurst College of today. Our founders had something special to preserve, protect, and advance. In Stanger's words, their goal was "to maintain a culture." Notice how carefully he refers to "*a* culture." The Reverend Kranz and the church fathers who sent him to Elmhurst would have been clear about what culture was to be maintained. Their particular challenge was to provide the

German settlements in the Midwest with educated clergy and teachers, men able to preach and pray in German and address the specific needs of their people.

The Elmhurst College of today serves a broad range of students, diverse in their ethnic backgrounds and their religious traditions, preparing to fill many different professional roles in a global economy. But we, too, aim at something special and distinctive. It is not our purpose simply to provide credentials in exchange for tuition. Our goal is much bigger and more important than that. The wilderness of our time may be more subtle, but it is too threatening to be ignored. Mindlessness, wastefulness, intolerance, hypocrisy, willful ignorance, self-righteousness, and greed stand in the way of our progress toward a just, inclusive, compassionate, responsible, and humane future. Elmhurst College is right here at the frontier, preparing strong men and women to think deeply, connect broadly, serve usefully, and live faithfully.

And what about those of us who are no longer college students? Of course we are attracted to that important mission and want to lend a hand to the next generation. But is there a broader message for our lives as well in that journey that brought Carl Kranz and his boys to Elmhurst? What about the wildernesses we find ourselves wandering through in our daily pilgrimage? There is the wilderness of complexity, when the strands of our lives become so entangled and the choices so impossible that there seems no way through the briars. There is the wilderness of sickness and pain when we or those we are close to feel the darkness closing in, and the sounds of the night bring fear rather than peace. There is the wilderness of loneliness and isolation that creeps up silently like a clinging vine and eventually closes off the path ahead.

From the perspective of their wilderness experience, the founders of America's early colleges had a particularly audacious idea that was at the same time supremely simple. As soon as you can, no matter what the challenges, make a little space in the wilderness for learning. There is no reason to assume that the principle works only for one kind of wilderness or only for one part of our lives. No matter our age or our circumstances, the fundamental facts apply. Following our curiosity where it leads, spreading our interests and our contacts widely, seeking ways to be useful to others, joining with others to think more broadly—these remain the pathways to growth and wisdom for as long as we want to stay vibrant and alive. Just as the pioneer college was a light in the wilderness of early America, so continued learning can be a light in the wilderness of our lives.

Our college's founders, like so many of those who created the early colleges of America, sought to light the lamp of learning in the darkness of the wilderness. We know they were clear about the ultimate source of that light by the Latin motto they chose for the College. You will find it in the official seal that is shown on the front of tonight's program. It is from a great Hebrew hymn of faith, Psalm 36: *In Lumine tuo videbimus lumen*—"In thy light shall we see light." Keeping that lamp of learning burning brightly remains our challenge today, and we are deeply grateful for all our friends who understand how important this is and who are ready to help keep Elmhurst College shining.

As we gather tonight, we are entering a season rich with the tradition of celebrating light in the darkness. It is something that has been a part of the human experience for a very long time—a warm, safe fire in the darkness of the winter solstice, a tiny jug of oil that kept a temple lamp burning through eight days and nights, a heavenly light that startled a group of humble shepherds on a dark hillside with a message of reconciliation and peace. Our holiday wish for each of you is that there may be light in your life, and that the days ahead may be particularly merry and beautifully bright.

SIXTEEN

The Big Promise of the Small College

THE OPENING COLLEGE RETREAT
AUGUST 21, 2000

Elmhurst College is one part of a large and complex system. All the colleges and universities that we usually think of as separate and independent institutions are, in fact, interlocking parts of a national and increasingly global network. Thinking of this network as an industry may help shed light on the challenges Elmhurst faces and the opportunities we have to carve out a special place in this system.

For those of us who care about colleges and universities, health care provides an instructive model of a somewhat similar industry in flux. A few decades ago, hospitals also thought of themselves as independent institutions, and many physicians practiced quite privately. Then health care costs rose dramatically, free enterprise moved in to provide a solution, and virtually every aspect of health care changed decisively. Some informed observers make the case that higher education is ripe for a similar process. Certainly, significant changes are going on in the industry in which we operate.

For example, the standing of traditional colleges and universities has been protected for a long time by certain boundaries. One such boundary has been the right to grant degrees. While anyone can teach a piece of content or a skill, only accredited public and (not-for-profit) private institutions traditionally have offered authentic degrees. Now, however, the largest growth area in postsecondary education by far is in the corporate sector, which bypasses traditional institutions altogether. Until recently, the boundary was an effective barrier. Now, the for-profit University of Phoenix—which recently made a major move into the Chicago area—is accredited by the same agency that accredits Elmhurst College.

Meanwhile, the traditional institutions with which we compete—for students, philanthropy, and attention—are hardly sleeping. We think of our campus as a more-or-less continuous construction site; but the prospective student who recently visited Millikin or Benedictine or Augustana, for example, saw more construction going on there than they found here at Elmhurst. For small private colleges, survival requires aggressive forward movement—and that lesson has been well learned by most of our competing colleagues.

And consider the heavily subsidized public sector. For many citizens of Illinois, the large state universities and community colleges offer attractive opportunities, and these institutions are competing vigorously. For years, some citizens of DuPage wondered why the county had no public four-year college campus. Then suddenly, without a centralized decision at the state or county level, Northern Illinois University built a new facility in Naperville, and the competitive environment for Elmhurst and the other small institutions in our area changed abruptly.

Thus, for those of us who care about the future of small colleges in general and Elmhurst College in particular, the current state of the higher education industry suggests a lot to worry about, and a lot to do in response. But I want to argue that we need to worry not just about what we will do, but also about what we would be.

We are a college, of course. There was a time when that was

the thing to be in higher education—when what we think of as the small liberal arts college was the typical place for an American to continue his or her education. But that time is long past. Someone has noted that the combined student bodies of the nation's elite liberal arts colleges could fit into the football stadium of any Big Ten university. In Illinois, only about 9 percent of undergraduates attend what we would call a small college. We need to recognize that the experience we offer is a rare one. If it lived in the wild, the kind of community we represent would be declared an endangered species.

A college that chooses to be called a college is even rarer. Most of our sister institutions are pursuing a different model. Perhaps they are responding to what George Dehne, a consultant on higher education, calls "the bigger is better trend." Benedictine, Concordia, Dominican, North Park, Trinity, Saint Xavier: these are all good small colleges in our part of the world—worthy competitors—who have adopted the name of university. Some folks have asked if that is the next logical step for Elmhurst, especially now that we offer seven master's programs.

Frankly, I hope not. At some point in the years ahead, we may conclude that it is unrealistic to fight the linguistic trend. When a culture changes the way it uses a word, it doesn't make much sense to insist on using the word in the old way and confusing everybody in the interest of a hidden purity. Still, I hope we will not be forced to change what we call ourselves, because I believe that the word "college" contains a rich set of meanings with important implications.

The word comes from the Latin *collegium*, carrying the idea of a group of individuals—colleagues—selected to serve together to accomplish a mission or purpose. Importantly, this is a created community, not a natural one, like a family. One becomes a member of a *collegium* by an appointment of a special nature. The root word *legare* means to appoint someone to carry out a charge. The prefix *co-* adds the notion that others share in the charge. Thus, the concept of a group of diverse individuals brought together to share a special mission is as close to us at this college as the word we use so lightly every day to describe what we are.

A second set of ideas embedded in the word has to do with the role of the college in the history of higher learning. In England, the endowed communities of learning around which Oxford and Cambridge grew used the college model. Beginning with Harvard in 1635, the model flourished in the United States, where the idea of a special space to gather together the future leaders of the community became part of the way life was organized, from the new cities to the advancing frontier. Only in the late nineteenth century was the university concept imported from continental Europe and superimposed on the distinctly American college. Yet the college was never completely swallowed up; the small-scale community for undergraduates survived in the United States as one of several different ways to organize a school.

In 1819 the model of the small private college was legally challenged, and then affirmed by the Supreme Court. Daniel Webster argued before the court that his alma mater, Dartmouth College, was a separately chartered institution, not a branch of state government that could be ordered about by the New Hampshire legislature. It is interesting to note that the specific act that led to the Dartmouth case was the legislature's attempt to unilaterally change the charter of Dartmouth to, among other things, rename it a university. Webster's famous closing argument captured well the special place the small college would have in the American consciousness:

Sir, you may destroy this little Institution; it is weak; it is in your hands! I know it is one of the lesser lights in the literary horizon of our country. You may put it out. But, if you do so, you must carry through your work! You must extinguish, one after another, all those greater lights of science which, for more than a century, have thrown their radiance over our land! It is, Sir, as I have said, a small College. And yet, there are those who love it.

So "college" is a word with a special heritage. That rich meaning finds expression in the current publications from our campus proclaiming that Elmhurst is "what college ought to be." That is a marketing declaration, but it is also a daily challenge. Can we make this place what a college ought to be? Certainly our small classes and the human scale of our activities and our campus give us a head start. But what is the potential we should be fulfilling?

We might draw inspiration from earlier attempts to define the possibilities of a college. Back in 1967, for example, Swarthmore College undertook a broad review of its work, which led to a remarkable document titled *Critique of a College*. One section is an examination of the implications of key characteristics of Swarthmore. What does it mean, for example, to be private, or coeducational, or selective? Finally, the authors turn to what it means to be a college, which they take to mean a small college.

First they distinguish themselves from a university, where the focus on faculty research and graduate students competes with attention to teaching and undergraduates. "Swarthmore's undergraduates are not second-class citizens, because the College is a classless society," the report states. "In an educational era when a great many students feel that they may be folded, stapled, or mutilated before they emerge from the educational sorting machine…the sense of being the focus of attention, and the point of the whole institution, can build morale and develop a sense of responsibility."

The report goes on to list the potential advantages of small scale to a college. I'll quote only the first sentences of a series of paragraphs:

- The small college has a high potentiality for close attention to students and quick response to their educational needs.

- The small college has a high potentiality for individualization of students' programs—for intellectual flexibility, and the development of self-direction.

- The small college has a high potentiality for achieving a connected education…not only [because] it is…easier to establish close relations among disciplines, but [also because] the college's intellectual life has a compactness that is lacking in larger institutions.

- The small college has a high potentiality for introducing students to new subjects and arousing their interests because of its accessible faculty.

- The small college has a high potentiality for encouraging students to learn from each other.

- The small college has a high potentiality for achieving a community beyond the curriculum.

- The small college has a high potentiality for innovation and experiment, since change ought to be possible on the initiative of a few people.

Note that the language is always of potential, which may or may not be realized. Our challenges at Elmhurst are different from their challenges at Swarthmore, but we share all of these possibilities. Potentially, we can model what a healthy intellectual community can be: "a free and ordered space," to use Bart Giamatti's fine phrase for thinking deeply about important matters while paying attention to and supporting one another.

I believe that as we work to respond to the challenges of our environment, we must find ways to assure that learning remains at the center of our enterprise. In this time of uncertainty for small colleges and for the entire industry of higher education, it is especially important to remind ourselves that learning is at the core of what we do.

Keeping learning at the center may help us manage the inevitable tensions between legitimate but conflicting ways to look at a college. If you ask a group of faculty and a group of students to describe how a college should work, you can expect to hear different perspectives. Faculty members are likely to emphasize what they do; to stress the importance of support for their scholarship and the value of self-reliant students. The students are likely to focus on what the college can do for them by providing options and opportunities, and to stress the value of faculty who respond effectively to student needs.

In his 1998 book *The Courage to Teach*, Parker Palmer contrasts the "faculty-centered model" with the "student-centered model." The first is likely to focus on academic rigor, says Palmer. The second is likely to produce calls for active learning. At their worst, he writes, such communities slip easily into "narcissism, where either the teacher reigns supreme or the student can do no wrong."

Most of us would want to get beyond the forced choice; and

in general, I think, Elmhurst does pursue a third way. We often refer to our college, appropriately, as "student-centered." But I wonder if the term we really are looking for is "learning-centered." Palmer suggests something similar in his book. "Perhaps the classroom should be neither teacher-centered nor student-centered but subject-centered," he writes. This is "a classroom in which teacher and students alike are focused on a great thing, a classroom in which the best features of teacher-and student-centered education are merged and transcended by putting not teacher, not student, but subject at the center of our attention."

The Swarthmore study made much the same point. "The finest colleges are those where the students and teachers form an intellectual community—that is, one bound together by a common enjoyment of learning and love of truth."

This passion for a subject, this devotion to learning, lies at the center of our life as a learning community. It is the passion of the scholar. As faculty at a small college, we model this commitment to learning, and we invite our students, one by one, to enter the company of scholars and share it with us. On a campus like ours, such a company must embrace not only the scholars who are teachers but also the scholars who are students. When faculty and students are colleagues, living the life of a company of scholars, then we are at our best as a college.

v *Our Community*

SEVENTEEN
The Persian Rubble

THE PRESIDENT'S BREAKFAST FOR
COMMUNITY LEADERS
MARCH 3, 2001

Welcome to the home of one of the best Division III men's basketball teams in the country, and one of the best collegiate jazz programs anywhere, and one of the best small college libraries in Illinois, and a place where day after day after day, we make a difference in the lives of students so that they can make a difference in the world. And, by the way, we do all these above-average things at a tuition level that remains below the average for private colleges.

I am particularly pleased to welcome you to this much-improved Frick Center. Elmhurst College students have gathered for meals at about this spot ever since 1871, first in the small farmhouse that was the entire campus at the beginning, then in a building called the Commons, which stood roughly in this location, then in the Student Union, which became the Frick Center, and now in this new and improved space. All those meals for all those years, all within a few yards of where we sit today. That steady evolution has reflected the institution's history and growth, and it reminds us of the everlasting interplay of continuity and change.

I want to think with you for a few minutes this morning on just that issue of continuity and change. Let's begin by going far back into history—all the way back to the ancient Greeks. It is 479 B.C., and the victorious Greek army is marching back into Athens. They have defeated the Persian army at the Battle of Plataea, but they are in no mood to celebrate. The soldiers have been dreading their first view of the Acropolis, that great hill that rises above Athens—*acro-polis*, the high city, where as far back as anyone can remember the gods have been worshiped in sacred temples. But now, having defeated the Persians, the Athenians have to face what their enemy had done to the Acropolis just before the battle. All the fine statues are gone, knocked over and smashed into pieces. One can hardly walk over the debris. Worst of all, the beautiful marble temple of Athena, not yet finished but already a graceful and elegant centerpiece of the hill, has simply disappeared. All that is left is the foundation, mostly covered now with marble slabs and stone drums that had once been pieces of columns. Instead of a fitting place to celebrate a great victory, here is a brutal reminder of the wages of war.

That first sight of their sacred Acropolis must have been shattering to those Athenian citizen-soldiers, but it was not a surprise. Messengers had brought them word about this terrible desecration. In fact, the hate that this destruction had inflamed in the army had driven them on during the battle. Just before the engagement, the historian Lycurgus tells us, all the Greek allies had sworn this oath:

> Of the shrines burnt and overthrown by the barbarians I will rebuild none, but I will allow them to remain as a memorial to those who come after of the impiety of the barbarians.

Over and over down through the ranks, the oath was repeated, with each man swearing to keep the memory of the desecration by the Persians alive forever by never rebuilding the temples of the Acropolis. Now the soldiers had returned to the sacred hill, victorious but absorbed by their great loss. Their fierce anger and their promise to the gods fresh in their minds, they walked back down to their homes and to their civic responsibilities to rebuild their lives under the shadow of the Acropolis, which they had sworn never to make beautiful again.

But of course, it was an arrangement that simply could not be sustained. Not with the surging energy of the Greek spirit; not with the strong leadership of a man like Pericles; and not with the way that great limestone crag of the Acropolis looms over Athens. Within a few years a dream had taken hold, and architects were at work on plans for a new and finer Acropolis, crowned by a new Temple to Athena, the Parthenon, built on the old foundation and following the same general design, but with a new level of refinement. This new building was to use traditional forms, a reminder of the temple that had been destroyed, but it would reach for new heights of perfection in balance and detail.

And yet there was the nagging matter of the oath. To the citizens of Athens, Pericles and his beautiful plans were one thing, but their sacred honor was something else. And it was not just the remembered words—there was the practical problem of the piles of consecrated stones resting just as the Persian barbarians had left them. Before the Athenians could proceed with the new building, there was the old question: "What shall we do with our past?" They found an answer to this enduring quandary, as every community must, though perhaps the answer itself is important to us only as it illustrates the seriousness with which they took the question.

Here is what they did. Gradually the hill was cleared, not by carting off the debris but by burying it. And not by the impersonal efficiency of just shoveling it under, but by carefully and with great piety laying out the remains of the sculpture and incorporating fragments of the old temple into the retaining walls around the now somewhat higher surface of the hilltop. In their own way, they kept their oath. They did not restore the old temple, and the shrines remained as a memorial. But they turned the debris into a platform on which to build. There can be little doubt that as the Athenians stood before their stunningly beautiful new temple forty years after the Persian destruction, they were keenly aware of the contents of the sacred ground on which they stood and the deep roots this wonderful building had in their own painful and glorious past.

Over the years, memories faded faster than the marble. The traditional religion declined; the temple was converted at one point to a Christian church and later to a Muslim mosque. And, of course, there was that disaster in the seventeenth century when ammunition stored in the Parthenon exploded, leaving the skeletal frame we nevertheless still revere as one of the finest buildings in history. But in the late nineteenth century, as archaeologists dug into the hill, they discovered—rediscovered really—what has come to be called the Persian Rubble. There under the surface, neatly organized, were the bits and pieces the ancient Athenians had so carefully saved for eternity—elements of the friezes from the older Parthenon laid out with obvious care, the beautiful statue of the calf bearer you can see now reassembled and restored in the Acropolis museum, and much more, a lot of it beyond easy recognition. The ancient Greeks, it turned out, had chosen not to ignore their past, but, with both decisiveness and reverence, to build upon it.

This audience does not need to be reminded that we live in an era of constant, rapid, and profound change. One of the subjects frequently identified as something future leaders need to study is "change management." We speak of successful institutions as those that are able to adapt to change. The shelves of books that are designed to help us deal with change range from heavy tomes from university presses with titles such as *Change Management Excellence: Putting Neuro-Linguistic Programming to Work in the 21st Century* to delightful little fables such as *Who Moved My Cheese?* Trying to keep up with this literature and the latest ideas about change is one of the challenges of contemporary culture.

But underneath all this attention to change and how we should respond to it is a relatively unexamined dimension that may perhaps be seen more clearly from the campus of a good liberal arts college. The human animal is not just a machine for adapting to external changes. People make decisions and choices that collectively influence the change around them, and people bring their past to every decision. Resistance to change is often rooted in complex stories that people remember. These stories may be woefully limited or inaccurate, but they are still powerful. In other words, people's first response to dreams for the future is very likely to be, "But what shall we do with our past?"

The Persian Rubble held the secret of how the Athenians of the fifth century B.C. managed to move from their past to their future, and perhaps it holds messages for us as well. First among them, it seems to me, is the importance of recognizing, respecting, and absorbing our past. In our formal education in America, we have tended to isolate the study of the past to a discipline called history, which has come to occupy a diminishing proportion of the curriculum. Colleges such as Elmhurst still insist on highlighting the study of history in our requirements, but we are consistently shocked by signs that young Americans, as the old Sam Cooke song says, "don't know much about history." Much more is involved here than just not doing well in a course in school. Ronald Reagan once put the issue in simple, straightforward terms. "If we forget what we did," he said, "we won't know who we are"—a particularly poignant remark from one who has since slipped into the fog of Alzheimer's. "If we forget what we did, we won't know who we are."

Let me give a small personal example of what happens when we add the past to the present. Not long ago I taught a senior seminar where a group of our best and brightest students focused on American higher education, its history, controversies, and future challenges. The first few days of the course were devoted to Elmhurst's own history, reading together the book *An Ever-Widening Circle: The Elmhurst College Years*, by Melitta Cutright. We talked about the wonderful stories from our past, about President Dinkmeyer, with no financial resources but with a serious need for a new residence hall, digging a big hole where Lehmann Hall now stands and putting up a sign: "A hole to be filled by faith." We looked at the old German inscription over the door of Old Main and remembered the years after World War II when those words were plastered over while the College wrestled with the complexity of its German heritage. One student's remark caught the flavor of what that experience did for the group. Now, she said, whenever she walks across campus, everything means something.

It is exactly that infusion of meaning into the present that the study of the past should be all about. What we need to encourage in this age that worships change is a constant awareness of what Mark Van Doren called "the connectedness of things." We can stand in front of Old Main and see only some words in a strange language, or we can recall that those words were carved when everything at the young school was being taught in German, that they were plastered over the year the College was suddenly filled with veterans returning from the war in Germany, that the plaster was cleaned off to display the writing again in more recent years at about the same time the College's special heritage took on an extra layer with the creation of the Holocaust Education Project. "The connectedness of things." When we live every day with this sort of continuity consciousness, we see things in multiple dimensions. Behind every artifact of today, we perceive its story over time. Those who do not take the time or make the investment to learn about the past are like an illiterate person looking at the daily newspaper. Seeing the type is not at all the same as seeing the meaning in the type.

Can't you imagine the Athenian citizen, showing off the new Parthenon to a visiting cousin from out of town, stopping to point out that there was so much more to understand than just some beautiful pillars? The old temple, the Persian destruction, the hard decisions, the sacred ground beneath their feet—all that was as much a part of what made the building so inspiring as the subtle curvature of the columns. Look at the whole thing, not just what the illiterate person might see. The first lesson of the Persian Rubble, then, is to embrace the past so that the present is infused with meaning.

But there is another side to the message of the Persian Rubble. It is embodied in that magnificent Parthenon. Even in its mostly ruined state today, we can see that this was no ordinary building. The grandeur of its concept and the subtlety of its execution put it in a class by itself. Just as the Athenian citizens were able to look at the Parthenon and see backward through layers of meaning, Pericles and his architects were able to look at the Persian Rubble and see forward to a level of excellence never before achieved.

This is the other side of continuity consciousness. What we do with the opportunities we have to make a difference in the world will help to shape the future. Not to know the past is a failure of understanding; not to dream of the future is a failure of vision. Both failures lead to an impoverished present.

The other day I was on another campus at the invitation of a president who wanted me to see a new performing arts facility that is nearing completion. As the architect took us through the hard-hat area, stepping over tools and material, he stopped over and over to explain something that wasn't there. Here in the lobby is where there will be a large piece of art that will add a note of grace and elegance. Imagine how these concrete walls will look when the warm wood panels and trim are installed. You can't see it now, but the flexible lighting in the hall will help it feel comfortable with different size audiences. And so on through the tour. I was interested in what I was seeing, but it was clear that for the architect, the reality in his head was far more important that what was visible to our eyes. And I must say, I have found myself doing the same thing over and over as I have shown people around this building. Understand that there is going to be a nice patio on the other side of these windows, that there is still more furniture that will be in those empty spaces upstairs. Imagine the flags of the countries from which our international students have come hanging around this room, adding color and meaning. And so on and on.

To look at what is and envision what could be is as important to the exercise of our full humanity as seeing through the present back into the past that explains it. And thus we have the two ways in which the consciousness of continuity enlarges our spirit and enriches our common life. If we had a ready way to measure it, we would no doubt find that most people's attention to the future is as shallow as their knowledge of the past. Just as we need to work at understanding our history, we need to give careful and disciplined attention to envisioning the future.

This is by no means just an abstract or academic exercise. Think of all the current issues that can be seen fundamentally as questions of how we understand the past and use them as a platform on which to build the future. The great economic decisions we are making as a people are—or should be—more than just short-term political deals. Can we get beyond simplistic and shallow theories of how we arrived at our current state of selective prosperity, and can we envision the future with clarity in a way that helps us make truly responsible choices now?

At the very local level, we will forever be faced with the dilemma of the teardown; history does not stand still. Can we see the human and relational community of which a particular building is only one element, and can we at the same time envision a future in which there will indeed be new buildings, but buildings of truly high quality that lift a community?

Look just across the street at the north end of Wilder Park and see if you can perceive—within the particular set of structures and streets there—the complex layers added from changing and conflicting perspectives over the decades of more or less unplanned transformation from farmland. But can you see also a thoughtfully created space where the mind and heart of the community are refreshed? Building the new library requires coming to terms with some Persian Rubble, but it is a magnificent dream worthy of a community's sacrifice.

Our big decisions—as individuals and as communities—always call in some sense for embracing and resolving our past while looking ahead to a created future. And that means that the quality of tomorrow depends on constantly replenishing the supply of people who are good at this. This is precisely what liberal arts colleges such as Elmhurst are all about. Our special mission is producing graduates who can see beyond the obvious to the important and who can imagine a better world and then help build it.

You who are friends and supporters of Elmhurst College are in a unique position to put your mark on the future by joining with us in this enterprise. All of us who work here are enormously grateful for your friendship. In return, may you take with you today the satisfaction of being associated with an institution that is doing something important, and may you find many ways in the coming weeks and months to infuse your life with a deeper understanding of the past and to enrich the world around you with your own dreams of a future yet to be built.

Making Music Together

REMARKS TO THE ELMHURST SYMPHONY ORCHESTRA
ANNUAL DINNER
JUNE 13, 2000

I would probably have said yes anyway, but I must say that when Mrs. Geraldi called to invite me to speak this evening, she gave me an assignment that was just too fascinating to turn down. We'd like to have you speak, she said, about the College and the community and how they are linked together by music.

Now on the surface, that seems easy enough. We all know that the Elmhurst Symphony Orchestra and Elmhurst College have a beautiful partnership. The orchestra has found a home at the College. The College, for its part, has found a way to give something back to the community by welcoming the orchestra and its audiences to its campus. This is a happy and healthy relationship and, indeed, shows the College and the community linked by music.

But somehow as the assignment has been rattling around in my head in recent days, it has seemed to me to stretch beyond just the fine arrangement these two community institutions enjoy. I found myself looking back at the history of how music has shaped the relationship between the College and the community, and I found myself looking forward to how important it is for all the major institutions in our community to make music together.

As a relative newcomer to the community myself, I am probably not in the best position to look back into its past. But I have learned something of the history of the College, and I have been impressed with how often music appears as a bridge between the campus and the surrounding community. I must begin by acknowledging that for much of its history, the College did not see the need to reach out to the community very much at all. Perhaps it was because the College had been founded by German immigrants who wanted to preserve their special culture, or perhaps it was all part of the strategy of isolating students from an environment that might entice them from their studies. Whatever the reasons, the College often seemed to turn inward. Look carefully at the buildings on campus and you will see that almost all of them face inward, away from the outside world. It is one of the things that gives the campus its intimate, enclosed sense. But when the College did turn toward the community, it was more often than not around music in some form.

Go back to the earliest years, and you will find one event each year where the outside world was invited in—a day each year called *Seminarfest*. This was a Sunday each spring when friends and supporters were invited to enjoy a picnic lunch, a few speeches, and lots of music. In 1888, so many came that two special trains were hired to bring the visitors from Chicago. While this event was eventually phased out as too expensive, it is the ancestor of the Summer Extravaganza that we will be enjoying later this month. Of course Maynard Ferguson is not quite the same as singing German hymns on the lawn accompanied by the College brass band, but music is a thread that unites them.

The College became serious about reaching out to the community during the short but important presidency of H. Richard Niebuhr, and the most dramatic step was the creation of a school of music in 1926, designed to offer music instruction for the community. In the announcement, Niebuhr wrote, "I believe the establishment of the school of music marks a new era of cooperation between town and gown." Over the years, many hundreds of Elmhurst children and adults have taken music lessons on campus—a tradition that continues to serve the community today.

And of course, the College's own musical groups have been ambassadors for the College for generations. Since the early decades of the twentieth century, choral groups from the College have been singing in churches and schools across the country and even around the world—this year they went as far as Poland. The wonderful Jazz Festival has been part of the local music scene since 1968. And for years now, the Elmhurst Choral Union and the College and Community Concert Band have brought amateur performers from around our area together to enjoy making music.

One of the great names of this tradition of music making is Stanger. We remember especially Robert Stanger, who served as president from 1957 to 1965 and gave so much to the community, including a dream he planted that some day the College and the community would build together a fine performance space. But before him there was his father, Christian Stanger, who taught music on the Elmhurst faculty for fifty years and was known as the leading organist of the area. That means that the name of Stanger has been associated with music in Elmhurst continually since 1896.

So in the history of the relationship between the College and the community, music has been much more than just a pleasant activity on the side. When College leaders sought ways to reach across the boundary between town and gown, they most often built the bridge with music. We still do.

But let's look a bit deeper into this business of building bridges with music. Perhaps there is a more profound meaning in the assignment I was given for this evening. What if we were to look not just at how music has been a bridge in the past, but at how making music shows us how to make all sorts of other bridges for the future? Perhaps the relationship between our two institutions—the orchestra and the College—can teach something about how all the different parts and major institutions of our community ought to interact and cooperate—that is, how we could all make music together.

Now, I am not really suggesting that we hand out instruments and scores to the City Council and the Park District and School District 205 and Elmhurst Memorial Hospital and the Chamber of Commerce and the Public Library and all the other institutions within the Elmhurst community and ask them literally to make music. I suppose if anyone could make something of such a hodgepodge of performers it would be Maestro Alltop, but it is highly unlikely the result would be particularly symphonic. No, I am suggesting that there is a rich metaphor here. When the orchestra and the College work together to make a concert possible, there are two sorts of music being made. There is the music we hear and enjoy from the stage, and there is the music of cooperation—the harmony behind the scenes that helps create something neither organization could create alone.

This idea that a community of people working together effectively is making a kind of music together is a very old one. Like many of our ideas of politics and community building, it has roots in ancient Greece. Students of the culture of fifth-century B.C. Athens have observed how intertwined music seems to have been with the whole idea of the *polis*—the political community. An appreciation of music and drama was expected of the good citizen. To be educated meant that one knew how to join in the rites and celebrations of the community and share its common culture as well as its debates and struggles. The goal was to belong to the chorus and thus participate in public life. Perhaps we feel a faint echo of this connection when we join at a public event in singing the National Anthem.

Society has long since left behind the notion of shared music as the essence of community life. Yet the metaphorical language is very much alive, and we speak of wanting to be on the same page as we seek harmony in our relationships. We want each person to have a voice, but we want our efforts to blend together.

There is more here than just poetic words. Working together to achieve a goal is the basic stuff of community building. But it doesn't come naturally and it often isn't easy. There is a superficial way to think of music that is a quite misleading model. Treating music as just sweet melodies and pretty harmonies makes it all sound easy. In fact, serious music is much deeper and more challenging than that. As the members of the orchestra will attest, making great music stretches both the physical and the mental capacities of humans to the limit. But making music together also stretches that other human capacity, the ability to learn to work together.

I've been reading a book about just this subject and I recommend it to everyone in this audience. It is by Arnold Steinhardt, the first violinist in the Guarneri String Quartet, and its title is *Indivisible by Four: A String Quartet in Pursuit of Harmony*. The Guarneri Quartet is a remarkable ensemble that has stayed together longer than any other major quartet in our time. They began performing together in 1965, and the same four are still together thirty-five years later. Their story demonstrates very clearly these two levels of music making we have been discussing. On the one hand, there is the wonderful elegance and passion of their playing—the music we hear in concert or on recordings. On the other hand, there is the human interplay as they struggle to work out the enormous range of agreements and compromises that allow them to thrive as a working group. When the title speaks of "the pursuit of harmony," it involves both these aspects and suggests that neither has come easily.

In fact, what may be a bit surprising about the book is that it is dominated by the struggles involved in this music behind the music. Here is how Steinhardt summarizes this difficult path to longevity:

> David Soyer is blunt and highly opinionated, John Dalley is sparing in his comments and often reserved, Michael Tree is an efficient problem-solver with an ebullient manner, and (please don't tell the others) I am a voice of reason and accommodation.... With four strong and somewhat fearless personalities, our road was much longer, more stressful, and, in the great tradition of democracy, exhilarating. What tempo should the opening of Mozart's "Dissonant" Quartet be? Is it wise to place the Mendelssohn A minor Quartet, which finishes quietly, at the end of a program? Should we accept less than our established fee for a concert offered us in Des Moines, Iowa, on a free day between engagements already booked in Chicago and Detroit? Each question elicited discussion, disagreement, and even occasional lost tempers. In the early years, I would sometimes return from a rehearsal dazed and exhausted by the continual process of conflict and resolution. But as we began to understand our differing tastes and individual ways of thinking through problems, our little democracy became more benign. David, Michael, and John weren't the enemy—they were just different from me. If the process of reaching agreement was slow and the outcome uncertain, at least it pushed you to think carefully about the important issues. There was strength in this ambiguity. And at some point during the ongoing rehearsals, discussions, struggles, and performances, the

individuals known as John Dalley, Michael Tree, David Soyer, and Arnold Steinhardt became the Guarneri String Quartet.

Music has brought us together tonight, and music has been the driving force that has made all your work worthwhile. We know what it means to struggle through our differences to achieve a goal we share. We know what it means to get over past hurts and disappointments in the interest of creating together something of quality. What our experience with making music teaches us is that the struggle itself is essential to our success. Music, after all, is all about the interplay of tension and resolution.

When the community of Elmhurst is at its best, it works this way. Of course there are conflicts. There are different concepts of the ideal outcome, and each institution within the community has its own self-interests. But if enough of us share a dream, and if enough of us concentrate on bringing our tensions to resolution rather than just proving our points, there is out there that tantalizing possibility that we could really make music together. The sign at the entrance to Elmhurst says, "A Proud Community." But proud of what? How about the music we make together? How about becoming a community known as a place where people and organizations cooperate and work together exceptionally well? I imagine some day in the future an exchange between two observers in a neighboring community that goes like this: "That Elmhurst is quite a place. How do they manage to do it?" "Well, I don't know, but they sure know how to make music together."

I hope the orchestra and the College will continue to model this approach for years to come. Music has often been the bridge that has brought the College and the community together. But the principle of living our community life as though we were making music together can keep us all achieving beyond what we now think to be our limits. Thank you for the opportunity to share this special evening. Thank you for all you do to provide Elmhurst with music for our ears and for our souls. And thank you for showing us all how to make music together.

Old Compass, New Ocean

ELMHURST ROTARY CLUB
ANNIVERSARY BANQUET
MARCH 10, 2005

S ome years ago I was at an antiques auction. The auctioneer was a masterful old fellow who had seen everything, and he maneuvered through the fast-paced action with the confidence of long experience. As he opened the bidding on a battered old grandfather clock, someone shouted from the back, "Does it work?" Without missing a beat, the auctioneer shouted back, "Does it work? Why, this clock worked years ago," and quickly returned to his auctioneer's chant and what soon became quite spirited bidding.

That answer is something to think about; it was, after all, "the truth"—sort of. But the *question* is one we all know well. It's as familiar as cleaning out your garage or attic. You pick up an old radio that was once the thing you reached for if you wanted music or news. Now it looks pretty bedraggled. But what is your first instinct? Of course, plug it in. Does it still work?

It is a question the early Chinese explorer Zheng He must have asked himself as he left the safety of the shoreline for a long ocean voyage in 1405, as far as we know the very first sailor to take along a curious little contraption with a magnetized needle to help him guide his ship on the open ocean. Now there was nothing new about the compass. That little toy had been in use in China for centuries as a trick used by fortune-tellers, and no doubt Zheng He had experimented with it in the harbor. But would it still work in a strange and dangerous new environment far beyond the horizon? Would the old compass work on a new ocean?

Life presents us with many situations where we ask just that question, "Does it still work?" We know the old way, the tried and true, the lessons we learned from the past. But will they work—are they still relevant—in a world so radically changed?

Rotary—both internationally and here in Elmhurst—has much to celebrate in this anniversary year. The saga of the rise and spread of the Rotary movement is itself convincing evidence that something must be working very well indeed. This particular club has done its part by helping to organize eight new clubs. It is also true that Rotary has changed and adapted over the years. Today it is a very different organization from that contemplated by the little group that Paul Harris met with in the office on the seventh floor of the Unity Building at 127 Dearborn back in 1905, and that evolution itself speaks to the continuing vitality of the institution.

Evolution and change and growth involve a constant reexamination of how we do things. Harris himself once wrote, "It is well that there is nothing in Rotary so sacred that it cannot be set aside in favor of things better." Anniversaries are times to celebrate success and memories of the past, but they are also good times to step back and reflect a bit, maybe even to make a resolution or two about how we want to face the future. So it seems to me that a part of such celebrations should be some time to consider the things that have made this experience valuable and how we might think of the meaning of Rotary as we look to the future.

In this spirit, I'd like to spend a few moments with you thinking about a particular set of words that are quite familiar to all members of the Elmhurst Rotary Club. Every time this club assembles you have a special ritual, and the piece of it that is the most different from the other service clubs in town is the recitation of the "Four-Way Test." Now rituals have a wonderful way of giving us a sense of permanence. After a few years of doing something the same way over and over, it's hard to imagine that there was a time when things were different. But in fact, the Four-Way Test is *not* celebrating its hundredth anniversary this year. It was introduced into the Rotary experience in the 1930s and in retrospect, it represented an attempt to bridge one of the great tensions within the Rotary movement, and within the traditions of most service clubs in America.

In a sense, Rotary had two beginnings. One was when Harris and his group of friends began getting together in each other's offices—rotating among them in fact—for fellowship and to help develop business relationships. The two objectives explicitly stated in the first constitution and bylaws adopted in 1906 were "The promotion of the business interests of its members" and "The promotion of good fellowship."

The first members were very serious about that matter of supporting each other's business, and in the early years one of the officers of each club was called the "statistician," with the job of keeping track of the business exchanges that developed out of club association. Certainly one of the reasons for the early restriction of choosing only one representative from each line of work was so that the members could boost each other's business without having to choose among competitors. It made a lot of sense to the four businessmen at that first meeting on February 23, 1905. As history would record, "Paul would buy his suits from Hiram, Hiram would purchase his coal from Silvester, Gus would use Paul for legal work, and so on."

But some months later, one of the early members,

Frederick Tweed, met with a friend, Don Carver, to ask if he'd be interested in joining. Carver, of course, asked what the club was for, and Tweed told him about those two purposes—boosting each other's business and promoting friendship. That just wasn't enough for Carver, who responded that he'd be more interested if the club "could do something of some benefit to people other than its own members." Tweed's response was exactly the right one for any club destined to evolve and grow. "Why don't you join the club," he said, "and perhaps we could amend the constitution the way you think it should be done." And a few months later, that's just what happened. The club was, in a sense, reborn, and the third purpose stated in the constitution became "The advancement of the best interests of Chicago."

Of course, that particular way of putting it turned out to be a barrier to be overcome when the idea of clubs in other cities came up, but at least the seed of the idea of service was planted. And with it was planted a tension that the great philosophers and ethicists have wrestled with through history. It is a dilemma I suspect many thoughtful Rotarians have turned over in their minds as well. "Am I here in this club primarily to advance my business and myself, or to help others?" One of the most interesting juxtapositions of the opposing principles occurred in 1910 and 1911, when the national conventions adopted two slogans at almost the same time: He Profits Most Who Serves Best, and Service Above Self.

So which was it to be? "I will serve others because I know I will benefit," or "I will serve others even if it conflicts with my personal interest"? The quick answer might be, "Why not both? Serve others, *and* it's okay if you benefit as well." But it's not that easy. Both statements are too definitive. According to the first motto, if you serve best, there is no alternative; you will be the winner. If, on the other hand, service is to be above self, then service clearly takes precedence—even if the interests of self are sacrificed. At some level, you really do have to choose, and my reading of what Rotary means to most Rotarians here in Elmhurst is that you are prepared to make the commitment and go with Service Above Self.

I think it's helpful to look at the history of the Four-Way Test through the lens of this tension and this choice. The story of the test is probably familiar to many Rotarians in this room. Herbert Taylor was a member of the Chicago Club—Rotary One—during the Depression, and in 1932, he was brought in to run a failing company and see if he could turn it around. The Club Aluminum Company was broke, and its employees were demoralized. The market for the high-quality cookware the company made had been cut by the terrible economic conditions, and competitors with better financing were capturing what was left.

Taylor decided that the company's best strength was the good character and integrity of its employees, and he set out to make these the company's competitive edge. After wrestling with—and praying about—the problem of how to help his employees understand the basic concept and keep it in their heads constantly, he came up with the words you recited earlier this evening. First he used the test privately for a few weeks, discovering that it helped him raise the right questions about his daily decision making. Then he had all his employees memorize it, and he and they did their best to apply it to all their dealings. Here is Taylor's analysis of the results, in his own words:

> The application of the Four-Way Test to our relations with our
> personnel and that of our suppliers and customers helped us to win
> their friendship and goodwill.... We have been rewarded with a

steady increase in sales, profits, and earnings of our personnel. From a bankrupt condition in 1932 our company within a period of some twenty years had paid its debts in full, had paid its stockholders over one million dollars in dividends, and had a value of over two million dollars.

Do you hear the echoes here of He Profits Most Who Serves Best? What if, in spite of his best efforts, Taylor had not succeeded in turning the company around? Would he have concluded that the test probably wasn't a very good idea after all? I don't think so. All I read about Taylor suggests he was a man of integrity and high standards, and my guess is he would have felt, in the end, that doing the right thing is the right thing even if one doesn't get rich by doing it.

Do you ever have the feeling, when you look back at history from the vantage point of our time, that you wish someone had handled things a little differently? The Founding Fathers were incredibly perceptive, but many of them just didn't see what slavery was doing to them. Don't you wish that, with 20/20 hindsight, we could go back and pull Mr. Jefferson aside and say, "Those words you wrote in the Declaration were right on; how about going back to your farm and really putting them into practice?" Well, I wish Mr. Taylor had not justified the fine principles in his test by the profit he felt he made from them, because they are the right principles, even without the profit—indeed, *especially* without the profit.

A small book written by Kent Keith makes the case in a unique way. It is titled *Anyway: The Paradoxical Commandments: Finding Personal Meaning in a Crazy World*, and some of you have no doubt seen it. Let me read a few of these "paradoxical commandments" to give some of their flavor:

- People are illogical, unreasonable, and self-centered. *Love them anyway.*

- The good you do today will be forgotten tomorrow. *Do good anyway.*

- Honesty and frankness make you vulnerable. *Be honest and frank anyway.*

- What you spend years building may be destroyed overnight. *Build anyway.*

- Give the world the best you have and you'll get kicked in the teeth. *Give the world the best you have anyway.*

I believe that somewhere deep down, most of us—and certainly most Rotarians—share the sense that true dedication to a cause is demonstrated most clearly when the principle is pursued in spite of great risk. In other words, in the last analysis we are defined by what we will do "anyway." If we really are serious when we say Service Above Self, we mean that even when it is inconvenient, even if we won't make the profit we had hoped for, we will serve others anyway. Not because we know we will come out ahead eventually; not because our company will be seen in a better light if folks know we do good things for the community, but simply because there is a serious human need, and responding to it is the right thing to do—anyway.

So here is my small contribution to the reflective component of your celebration of fifty years of Rotary here in Elmhurst. The next time you recite the Four-Way Test, take just a moment to remember the difference between doing good so that you or your firm will make a profit, and doing the right thing because it is the right thing.

- Is it the truth? Whether there is profit in it or not, I am going to be trustworthy anyway.

- Is it fair to all concerned? Whether my company prospers or not, I am going to stand for justice and fairness in my circle of acquaintances and in my community anyway.

- Will it build goodwill and better friendships? Whether people think I'm a little crazy or not, I am going to build friendships across boundaries and I am going to be there for all my friends anyway.

- Will it be beneficial to all concerned? Whether anyone else notices or not, even if it means giving up some of my leisure time, even if it leaves me not quite as rich as I was, I am committed to service above self. So I am going to serve extravagantly so that there will be benefits to go around for everyone. And by the way, those are benefits for *others*.

Does the Four-Way Test still work? You bet it does. But not in the way Herbert Taylor thought it would. When we put on the clear, sharp reading glasses of the standard of Service Above Self, we see the familiar words for what they could mean—for what they ought to mean. The old compass works on our complex ocean, but only if we read it from the right perspective. Its job is not to tell us our fortune but to help us stay pointed toward our purpose.

Rotary has grown and matured over the hundred years of its life and over its fifty years here in Elmhurst. One strand of that growth was the expansion of its mission beyond just growing our businesses to a deep commitment to serving others. Another change, perhaps more subtle and hidden, has been the gradual movement away from the principle that we serve others because in the long run it's good for us and our business, and toward the realization that our calling is higher than that. Rotary serves because there are people with desperate needs. Rotary makes a difference in our community because there are important things to be done here—Elmhurst needs Rotary. The world is full of hurt and tragedy and lost opportunity and places where the human fabric is ripped and torn. Rotarians are people who say—every week when they are together and every day in their lives—Service Above Self. Whatever the challenges of the next fifty years, no matter how tough the problems we face, may Rotary always be there—yes, enjoying good fellowship, and even helping each other succeed in professional endeavors. But in the last analysis and when the chips are down, may Rotary always be there, putting Service Above Self, *anyway*.

V OUR COMMUNITY

The Art of Associating

O ne hundred and seventy-four years ago today—in the year
1831—two young men were in the final weeks of preparing
to set sail across the Atlantic to visit the New World. They were in
their mid-twenties and had grown increasingly unhappy with the
latest regime change in their native France, as it struggled through
the years following the Revolution and the rise and fall of Napo-
leon. They had managed to secure leaves of absence from their
government jobs by proposing to study the American approach
to running prisons, something their supervisors found especially
interesting. But in fact, they had a bigger idea in mind. One of
the young men, Gustave de Beaumont, wrote to a friend:

> We contemplate great projects; first we will accomplish as best we can
> the mission given us…but, while doing the penitentiary system, we
> will see America…. Wouldn't a book be good if it gave an exact idea
> of the American people, showed their history in broad strokes, painted
> their character in bold outline, analyzed their social state, and rectified
> so many of the opinions which are erroneous on the point?

Well, eventually a book did emerge, and indeed it was good;
but it did not come easily. First there was the journey itself—
nine months of adventures. They enjoyed the social life of
Boston, New York, and Philadelphia. They put up with arduous

travels through terrible weather to New Orleans and west to the Michigan wilderness. They made lots of short stops along the way—to celebrate the Fourth of July in Albany, to inspect prisons in Auburn and Sing Sing, to recover from a steamboat crash near Wheeling, to visit Cleveland and Cincinnati and Detroit and Niagara Falls. They had hundreds of interviews with business leaders, lawyers, common laborers, and even President Andrew Jackson. They met with the only signer of the Declaration of Independence who was still alive, Charles Carroll of Maryland.

What they saw and heard captivated them, but the immensity and complexity of America overwhelmed them as well. The "great project," as they called it, would be more challenging than they had imagined. The younger man, a well-educated aristocrat named Alexis de Tocqueville, wrote home, "I hope that we will do something good here. However we must not flatter ourselves yet. The circle seems to expand as fast as we advance." And then comes the comment we professors have heard from students all too often, "We have not yet written a line, but we are accumulating a great deal of material."

It did not get any easier after their return to France. First there was that report on the American prison system to complete. Then began the long struggle to think through what their experience had meant and, particularly, what general principles might be derived. After all, they had not undertaken the trip out of any particular love of America, but rather to learn what they could about where European politics might be heading. By 1835, Tocqueville was ready to publish the first part of their study. It was quickly translated into English, and *Democracy in America* began its life as the most famous examination of America by a visitor and one of the most important studies ever of how democracy works.

Tocqueville's book is, in short, a classic. Now a classic may be defined as a book you feel guilty for not ever having actually read. In fact, I suspect many in this room *have* read at least snippets of *Democracy in America* at some point for some class or other. A less cynical definition of a classic is a book that is worth reading again. A great book grows with us, and we can sometimes be amazed at how much more is in it than we saw the last time. Someone once said that when you read, "the book reads you." Many of the great books probably did not find us very interesting reading when we were eighteen or nineteen, but it might be different now. So if you have a chance sometime to sit down with a copy of *Democracy in America* and read from the sections that interest you, you are likely to enjoy a fascinating conversation with an extraordinary visitor with whom you will sometimes agree and sometimes want to argue.

Tocqueville's great theme was how America embodied and played out the idea of equality. Without an entrenched aristocracy, people were freer to make their own way, with their fortunes rising and falling according to their own resourcefulness. Democracy is simply the political outcome of equality, and Tocqueville uses the terms almost interchangeably. Equality of condition, he argues, is a principle that is destined to spread through other lands as well, though different nations are likely to experience the transformation differently.

Tocqueville finds much to praise in America, but the work as a whole is not totally optimistic. Embedded in the notion of equality and democracy are serious risks, he argues, and the liberty and well-being of future generations will depend on how the great experiment proceeds. The challenge ahead—for America, for Europe, and even for readers of today—is how to reinforce what is positive about democracy while countering its very substantial risks.

The gravest of these risks, according to Tocqueville, is that the will of the majority becomes the only final authority, and that if left unchallenged, it might become as despotic as any king, although in new ways. In one of the most passionate sections of the book, he discusses how freedom of thought and conscience can survive the physical punishments of a tyrannical king but not the more subtle pressures exerted by a majority with its mind made up.

> A king's only power [was] material…it [affected] actions but [had] no way of influencing wills. In the majority, however, is vested a force that is moral as well as material, which shapes wills as much as actions…. Under the absolute government of one man, despotism tried to reach the soul by striking crudely at the body; and the soul, eluding such blows, rose gloriously above it. Tyranny in democratic republics…ignores the body and goes straight for the soul.

Tocqueville's observation is worth pondering in our time. From a national perspective, it may not always be quite clear where the majority is; for example, at the moment there appears to be a fairly even division of political opinion on many issues. But the daily lives of most of us are lived in the context of local majorities. The country as a whole may be divided, but people live in blue states or red—blue towns or red. Chicagoans root for the Bears and Philadelphians root for the Eagles. Almost everyone lives surrounded by some form of majority opinion, and perhaps our era is best thought of as a time of competing majorities. Tocqueville reminds us that the great cause of reinforcing the good side of democracy is not well served by insisting that all right-thinking people should follow the majority and those who don't should be marginalized. Rather, democracy is nurtured by independent thinking, by challenging prevailing opinion, by vigorous debate, and by listening with an open mind to those with different perspectives.

Of course, this is a book that deserves a course or two of study, not just a few brief after-breakfast remarks. But I think Tocqueville does have something special to say to us in this particular setting this morning. He and his friend never got as far as Elmhurst in their travels, and they wouldn't have found much here in the 1830s if they had. But if they were to visit today, they would surely notice a good deal of supporting evidence for a particular section of *Democracy in America*. In part 2 of volume 2, Tocqueville explores one of the most troublesome possible outcomes of equality of condition, namely, an excess of individualism.

When people view themselves as essentially equal, Tocqueville argues, they are more inclined to forget the responsibilities they owe each other and withdraw into their own narrow circle of family and friends. But sustaining democracy requires involvement and commitment to the common welfare. Tocqueville saw two special ways that Americans counteracted this natural tendency toward too much individualism. The first was the decentralization inherent in the federal system, where local matters are attended to by local government. "When citizens are forced to concern themselves with public affairs," he writes, "they are inevitably drawn beyond the sphere of their individual interests."

But the second counterbalance to excessive individualism is not political at all. Nevertheless it is, in Tocqueville's view, the foundation for preserving liberty, and it was the thing that most amazed him in his travels. Americans associate—and in extraordinary ways. Listen to his glowing words on the subject:

> Americans of all ages are constantly joining together in groups. In
> addition to commercial and industrial associations in which everyone

takes part, there are associations of a thousand other kinds: some religious, some moral, some grave, some trivial, some quite general and
others quite particular, some huge and others tiny. Americans associate
to give fêtes, to found seminaries, to build inns, to erect churches,
to distribute books, and to send missionaries to the antipodes. This
is how they create hospitals, prisons, and schools.... Wherever there
is a new undertaking, at the head of which you would expect to see
in France the government and in England some great lord, in the
United States you are sure to find an association.

He goes on to examine why "associating" is so critical to the
success of democracy and why Americans seem to have become
so good at it, and then concludes:

Of all the laws that govern human societies, one seems more precise
and clear than all the rest. If men are to remain civilized, or to become
so, they must develop and perfect the art of associating to the same
degree that equality of conditions increases among them.

"They must develop and perfect the art of associating." And
that, my friends, is where you come in. Every person in this room
is involved in just the sort of associations that Tocqueville found
so amazing. Now I doubt that "amazing" is a term most of us
most of the time would apply to the chores and responsibilities we
volunteer for or let ourselves get talked into. But each of us could
assemble quite a list. Think for a moment of yours. There is the
church, the service club, the bowling league, the health club, the
garden club, the book group, the investment club, the nonprofit
board, the chamber, the library association, the neighborhood
association, the golfing buddies, and then of course, the things
we've cycled in and out of as our family has grown—the PTA,

the soccer league, the scouting group, and on and on. And add to that the great hobby called "local government" that draws us into another layer of meetings and commitments.

A few years ago Robert Putnam made a big splash with a book called *Bowling Alone*, in which he argued that Americans are fast becoming loners who have withdrawn from shared activity, thus reducing the nation's "social capital." But there is a good deal of countervailing evidence about the increase in volunteering and the morphing of associations into new and sometimes less visible forms. In any case, Putnam was certainly not talking about the people in this room.

No, the challenge before *us* is the one posed by Tocqueville—the development and perfecting of "the art of associating." How can each of us get better and better—and help our colleagues and neighbors get better and better—at this business of working together to advance the common good? I think we can find some hints in Tocqueville's observations, some principles that might give us guidance.

First, and perhaps most fundamentally, there must be a deep commitment to the *common* good. The pattern of civic involvement Tocqueville was used to seeing in traditional Europe was an individual, seeking some benefit for himself or herself, going to a government official to seek assistance. What he saw in America, at its best, was people identifying a common, shared benefit, and then coming together to make it happen. "I am bound to say," he writes, "that I have often seen Americans make large and genuine sacrifices to the public good, and I have noted on countless occasions that when necessary they almost never fail to lend one another a helping hand." We nurture the democratic spirit, in other words, when we define the purposes of our associations in terms of what is best for the whole community, as opposed to the pursuit of a private interest.

Sacrificing for the common good does not come naturally, so part of our job is to push people's understanding of what is worth achieving to a higher level. This is a particular challenge, I think, for leaders acting as representatives of others. Yes, we are there to fight for the interests of our constituents, but we are just as responsible for helping to raise the sights of our constituents to a higher, broader understanding of what is best for the whole community and across boundaries.

A second guiding principle is civility. Tocqueville gives a great deal of attention to manners, and at first we might think this just a natural reflection of his aristocratic upbringing. But it goes much deeper than that. What he is getting at is the way we advance the spirit of democracy by respecting others, by being generous and thoughtful, and by seeking out ways to cooperate in friendship. For example, he demonstrates why local elections, even though they might divide people temporarily, ultimately ought to encourage civility. A leader at the national level, he says, might easily sway voters with some popular decision, but—in words that might serve as good advice to all local politicians—Tocqueville says that "to earn the love and respect of one's neighbors takes a long series of small services and obscure favors, habitual and unremitting kindness, and a well-established reputation for impartiality." "A long series of small services," "habitual and unremitting kindness"—that is "the etiquette of democracy" on which so much depends.

Finally, there is the guiding principle of leadership. On the surface, Tocqueville seems to give little direct attention to leadership. He was more inclined to see the many people coming together than to focus on those who were doing the work of pulling them together. Or perhaps he simply understood how broadly leadership needs to be spread around if democracy is to work. And so he writes:

> In America I came across types of associations which I confess I had no idea existed, and I frequently admired the boundless skill of Americans in setting large numbers of people a common goal and inducing them to strive toward that goal voluntarily.

This "boundless skill" is in fact something all of us need to work on constantly. Fortunately for us, we live in an era in which leadership has been explored and dissected, and the basic attributes of effective leadership have been spelled out and can be studied. What is important is to take the leadership of all our many associations seriously and to commit ourselves to the hard work of becoming ever more skillful at "setting large numbers of people a common goal and inducing them to strive toward that goal voluntarily." That's as good a definition of leadership as I know.

Tocqueville never returned to America. He lived a life of scholarship and engagement, maneuvering the twists and turns of French politics, serving in the Legislative Assembly and even briefly as minister of foreign affairs. But what he left us was a masterpiece from which Americans can still learn. You are visiting today a college where he is still read and where our future leaders are being prepared. It is a college committed to helping its students develop a passion for the common good, the etiquette of democracy, and the skills of leadership so that they will make their own contribution to the renewal of the democratic spirit in their time.

Now is the time to thank everyone here this morning for your support and encouragement of this important enterprise, and to wish each of you all the best as you work day by day to be the best possible practitioners of "the art of associating."

VI *Simple Things*

Seeking Simplicity

THE PRESIDENT'S HOLIDAY DINNER
DECEMBER 13, 1998

T his is a time of year when life gets complicated. Our social calendars fill up with festive events to the point where we have to run from one to the other and check to see if we're still having fun. That special day when we will want to have gifts ready for our family and friends looms like a deadline. The year-end tax deadline approaches as well, as we wonder if we have done all we should have with the management of our finances for the year. The crowds and the insistent noise of department store carols put our nerves on edge. And this year, an appalling and tragic drama is playing itself out in Washington and across the country as a surreal sidebar to the season.

It is almost as though someone installed the twelve days of Christmas in some giant computer and programmed it to spin out of control, giving us thirteen schedule conflicts, seventeen people unhappy with something we haven't done, and one hundred fifty-eight more things to worry about.

But now and then, if we are lucky, we sense nearby, even if just out of reach, a small candle flame, a fleeting moment, of peace. Perhaps it is a particularly quiet moment, perhaps a small fragment of beauty in music or nature; perhaps we find an answer to a vexing problem, or a question is framed for us in a fresh way that gives new focus to our thinking. A common characteristic of those moments is the sudden sense that it's really not so complicated after all.

A while back, when I was fretting with my wife Jeanette about tonight's event and what I could possibly say that would be at all appropriate, she said—right out of the blue with no preparation—"'Tis the gift to be simple." On reflection, I'm not sure whether she meant it as a suggested topic or as a gentle reminder that the occasion calls for brief after-dinner remarks rather than the complicated philosophical lecture she was afraid I might be planning. But her reference to the old Shaker song struck a chord that has been reverberating in my thinking this Christmas season.

I'm sure you would all recognize the tune if I had the nerve to sing it, and you would hear in it the purity of country air that the composer Aaron Copland captured when he used the melody as the theme of his *Appalachian Spring*. The Shaker songbooks of the 1840s and '50s called it "Simple Gifts."

> *'Tis the gift to be simple,*
> *'Tis the gift to be free,*
> *'Tis the gift to come down*
> *Where we ought to be.*

Simplicity that takes us where we ought to be. What a perfect antidote to the disease of too much—too much to do, too many things to buy and dispose of, too many choices, too much clutter in our lives—what one writer calls "affluenza." What a gift—and yet what a difficult and complicated goal simplicity turns out to be. There is no shortage of advice. Check out the shelves of any large bookstore and you will find detailed instructions about how to simplify your life with a planner in which you write your schedules and your lists—followed, of course, by your list of lists. And then you will find Elaine Saint James, who has made a career of writing books about simplification, telling how the first thing she did to simplify her life was throw away her planner. If you'd like, you can even join another organization and subscribe to a magazine called the *Journal of Voluntary Simplicity*.

Yet for all its challenge, we cling to the dream. We know intuitively that Thoreau was right about our lives being "frittered away by detail," and we relish the opportunities we do have from time to time to spend a quiet evening with a book, or relax with a true friend, or do some piece of work with our hands that reminds us of simpler times.

But I wonder how often we link our urge toward simplicity to the enterprise of education that brings us together here at Elmhurst College? Usually, learning seems the very opposite of simplicity. Is not the object to learn more and more about increasingly complicated subjects? After all, we know that when students finish college, we give them a degree we sometimes call a B.S.—and we all know what that means—and then we invite them to add an M.S., which stands for more of the same, and then, if they want to go even further, they can pursue a Ph.D.—piled higher and deeper.

It's true that one of the biggest drivers of education is curiosity to learn more and more. But underneath this is the more profound truth that the search for understanding is fundamentally an attempt to find *simpler* explanations. A moment's reflection will confirm that unifying and simplifying is what scholarship is really all about. We can enjoy one by one the millions of birds that share our environment. But we begin to *understand* when we realize that all those bright red birds are in fact closely related, and that it's far simpler to describe the common traits of the cardinal than to try to learn about every red bird, one by one. Then there is the economist who tries to gain the clearest possible insight into the huge number of transactions among people by proposing the simplest possible set of principles by which they can be understood. Albert Einstein's extraordinary accomplishment was to find an incredibly simple geometric explanation for the relationships among time, space, and gravity.

And so it goes. Learning is not a matter of accumulating more and more random and unrelated bits of information. We learn by constantly developing better and more satisfying simplifications of the buzzing and whirring confusion around us. Ultimately, it is dissatisfaction with our current understanding—our current simplification of reality—that drives us to want to learn more. And here we come to the great dilemma and the great trap of learning. We learn to become more satisfied with our understanding, but we are at the greatest risk of error when we achieve satisfaction. It is when we are sure that we know the final, simple answer and we stop seeking a better understanding that our minds atrophy and our hearts grow hard. That is why the most interesting and inspiring people are those who are searching for the truth and the most dangerous are those who have found it.

The great mathematician and educator Alfred North Whitehead put it this way: "Seek simplicity, and distrust it." The educational mission that we are about here at Elmhurst—and, I hope, the learning all of us here tonight pursue as we continue to grow in our daily lives—is all about seeking a clearer, simpler grasp on life in all its complexity. But it absolutely requires the open mind and inquiring spirit that has no patience with self-righteousness. This commitment to keep learning—to keep seeking simplicity—is at the core of liberal education. T. S. Eliot gives us this reminder for those times when we are tempted to close our eyes and ears to new challenges: "There is more to understand. Hold fast to that as the way to freedom."

So simplicity turns out to be far more than just reducing the clutter of our lives. We are seeking simplicity when we try to understand chemical bonding or the causes of the First World War. We are seeking simplicity when we try to come to grips with what is truly going on in national politics today. We are seeking simplicity when we open our minds to poetry and to art. We are seeking simplicity when we wrestle with the mysteries of faith and the demands of personal responsibility.

And when we gather round this great College and cheer it on and help to assure its health and vigor, we are giving precisely that gift. Without support from people like you, Elmhurst College would long ago have slipped into obscurity and probably oblivion. With your support, we are showing another generation of students what it means to think, to create, to serve, to seek simplicity, and, yes, to distrust it. For that, they and I are immensely grateful.

I hope in return that each of you will find some simple gifts during this special season—simple gifts that help to take you where you ought to be.

In the midst of the noise and the rush of too much to do, may you find some moments when you can be alone with your own silence.

In the season of crowds and traffic jams and big parties, may you have some peaceful time with the few people who mean the most to you.

As a supporter of education, may you have the chance to learn something new yourself, read a book that intrigues you, or enjoy some music or art or drama that speaks to you with insights simple and profound.

In this time of poisoned politics, may you find the simple wisdom to tell the difference between the words that must be said and the rhetoric of destructive hatred.

In this holy time, may you have some interval of spiritual refreshment when you can listen for that still, small voice.

As you seek simplicity yourself, may you find a way to share some simple anonymous gift with someone who has no reason to expect an act of kindness from you.

And, finally, may you catch a glimpse of that ultimate simplicity that is beyond understanding—what we call mystery: the mystery of a child, the mystery of God's great love, and the miracle of joy.

Thank you for joining us this evening; thanks for your support of Elmhurst College; and our very best wishes to you for a simply wonderful holiday season.

What the Silence Is For

THE PRESIDENT'S HOLIDAY DINNER
DECEMBER 4, 2005

A ll of us who have spent time as teachers—or parents, for that matter—know the feeling of discovering something that works—some approach that clears the way for a youngster to learn. For Randy Howe, a special education teacher in New Haven, Connecticut, one of those moments came as he worked with a third-grade girl with cerebral palsy. She was a bright and hard-working child who would probably never be able to talk. With the school's speech therapist observing his work, Howe struggled to teach her to communicate with picture cards. When he feared that the long pauses in her responses were undermining her confidence, he would prompt her and try to help her along. No, said the therapist, you have to wait. "The learning happens in those uncomfortable moments. That's what the silence is for."

"That's what the silence is for." The lesson the young teacher learned that day is that silence is not just the absence of sound or activity—not just empty time; in the right context, silence might become a special space within which a student can learn. How is it that apparent nothingness can become something so substantial and so powerful? What else might silence be for? What might the quiet times mean in our lives? What are the uses of quietness?

A good place to begin is with the assumption that silence is nothing—as opposed to sound and activity, which represent something happening. What if we were simply to reverse the polarity and think of silence as the natural state and noise as an interruption—perhaps sometimes a violation—of that state. This would, in fact, have been the easiest assumption until very, very recently. Looking back on the long sweep of the history of humankind on the planet, the years of the last century or so have been uniquely noisy. It's hard for us even to imagine a time without electronically reproduced voices and music, without the rumble of motor vehicles, without the clatter of machinery of all kinds. But I think if we were suddenly transported back to, say, the early days of our country, one of the first things that would hit us would be its relative silence. The Swiss philosopher Max Picard has written this about silence:

> Nothing has changed the nature of man so much as the loss of silence. The invention of printing, [technology], compulsory education— nothing has so altered man as this lack of relationship to silence, this fact that silence is no longer taken for granted, as something as natural as the sky above or the air we breathe.... Man is not even aware of the loss of silence: so much is the space formerly occupied by the silence so full of things that nothing seems to be missing.

A first thing that times of quietness can do for us is to pull us away—even if only temporarily—from the noise of our modern world. In 1955—fifty years ago this past spring—the Commencement Address at Elmhurst College was delivered by one of her greatest sons. H. Richard Niebuhr had graduated forty-three years before that, had served a critical few years as president of the College, and had then gone on to a prestigious professorship at Yale and a reputation as—along with his older brother Reinhold—one of the twentieth century's most important theologians. He found his inspiration for the address in the words of Isaiah: "In quietness and in confidence shall be your strength" (Isaiah 30:15). He spoke of "the noisy century" that had moved from horse and buggy to jet planes and was now filled with grinding gears and laboring engines, the thunderclap of broken sound barriers—even atomic explosions. But the enduring work of the world, he said, goes on in quietness—the work of peace making, the work of healing, the work of science, the work of wisdom, the work of suffering, the work of soul making.

Thomas Merton, the Trappist monk whose spiritual journey has been an inspiration to so many, also wrote of this need to find a way out of the noise of modernity. He argued that it is all too easy to allow our lives to become so filled with the clutter of diversions that we lose our sense of ourselves. "The function of diversion," he wrote, "is simply to anesthetize the individual as individual, and to plunge him in the warm, apathetic stupor of a collectivity which, like himself, wishes to remain amused." And he was writing before the arrival of that great little iPod that enables us to carry musicians around in our pocket and encase ourselves in a personalized sound track for our daily lives. The new marketing slogan of Tower Records says it all: "Life Played Loud."

Quiet times, then, are times of rest and relief, of stepping away from the cacophony of a noisy world, of reconnecting to our humanity and our identity. Such times are valuable because they are rare and must be consciously sought. The fact that it is so hard to find time for quietness is precisely why we should.

But a special thing happens as the noise level is reduced; our ears become sharper. And that brings us to the second thing that silence is for; quiet times are especially suited for listening. It seems, in fact, that we listen best in silence. In our quiet times, we can listen to ourselves and work on the inner integrity on which all else depends. In Thomas Merton's words, silence is a place where we "realize who we are, who we might be, and the distance between these two." In quiet moments, we can listen to others—our friends, our loved ones, and those who are voiceless, those near and far whom we so easily overlook in the hustle and bustle of everyday life. And best of all, in the silence we can listen for that still, small voice of the Great Mystery. When the psalmist took the time to listen, the words he heard were, "Be still, and know that I am God."

There is, of course, a kind of silence in which we avoid listening. It is the unhealthy silence that forms between two people who were once close but who have let themselves drift into private worlds. The poet Ric Masten captures this breakfast-table scene:

> *Robert....*
> *Buried in the* Tribune *with his coffee.*
> *Reading all about the day before.*
> *Nancy....*
> *Just across the table with her teacup.*
> *Studies what the tea leaves hold in store.*
> *And the now,*
> *The moment slips away.*
> *Gone with its joy and sorrow.*
> *He was here yesterday*
> *And she is coming tomorrow.*

But when we are listening for each other's voice, there can be quiet times together in which words are not necessary—"two people together but alone, quietly recharging."

So quietness is for rest and refreshment in a hectic world, and quietness is for listening—*really* listening. And finally, as the young teacher discovered, quietness is for learning. We educators tend to work hard at the parts of teaching we can control. But the breakthroughs often come when a student wrestles with a problem alone. Those long hours in the library, the laboratory, or the studio are times when information is processed, when bigger ideas click into place. We all need the stimulation of human interaction that challenges and encourages. But discovery, invention, and creativity, inspired in community, germinate in solitude.

And how desperately our public life needs citizens willing to take the time to step out of the whirlwind of blaring propaganda and battling sound bites to think quietly for themselves. The color of truth appears to have been reduced to either red or blue because people with a stake in our believing that have told us so. Citizenship in a democracy demands more than just the pursuit of political advantage. Taking the time to study, to inquire, to listen most carefully to that which we most fear, to test our conclusions against the deepest principles we know—this requires quiet time for serious reflection. It is what Niebuhr spoke of fifty years ago as the work of peace making, the work of healing, and the work of wisdom that are the fruits of quietness.

So the quiet times of our lives are not empty spaces, time wasted because it is not filled with busyness. We need those times to save us from being swept away in a tide of noisy distraction and to help us listen and receive; and if we choose, we can use those times to open windows to learning, creativity, and insight. That's what the silence is for.

We are entering now a special season of celebration. It will be a busy time, full of things to be done and places to be, with joyful noise throughout. But there has always been a thread of silence running through this time of year—the long, still hours of darkness as the little flask of sacred oil burned on for eight nights; the quiet hillside where shepherds heard a whisper of heaven; the snow-covered serenity of the winter solstice. In the early nineteenth century, when a young German pastor tried to capture in a simple song the very essence of the Christmas story, it turned out to be "*Stille Nacht*," Silent Night.

What better time of year to seek some quiet moments? A long walk in the winter stillness, perhaps, or a quiet hour with a friend over a gentle cup of coffee, or a peaceful evening by a warm fireplace. For the Carmelite nun and poet Jessica Powers, silence was the pathway to revelation. In "The Christmas Silence," she wrote:

> *Here in the cloister they who seek discover*
> *A wandered fragment of the Christmas silence*
> *That hid itself from the disquieted earth:*
> *The silence of the Virgin bending over*
> *The little Uncreated Innocence*
> *Upon the bed of a most hidden birth,*
> *The silence that was Joseph's sacrament*
> *Through years that were a threshold to this hour....*
>
> *They who go walking in the Christmas silence*
> *Through any season of the changing year*
> *Come to a Man with peace upon his brow*
> *And see the Mother and the Infant near.*

Many fine gifts will be given and received during this season. I hope that one of them for each of you will be some quiet time. The College you support with your friendship is a vibrant place that is often busy with activity and energy as all of us involved learn and grow. But at Christmastime our campus will become very quiet. I hope you too will find moments when you are able to step away from all the bustling activity and all the noise of our time and find, even if only briefly, a fragment of the Christmas silence to refresh your soul. That is our holiday wish for each of you.

TWENTY-THREE

Let's Talk

THE PRESIDENT'S BREAKFAST FOR
COMMUNITY LEADERS
MARCH 6, 1999

I t's always a pleasure to welcome back to the campus this wonderful group of people who are willing to come out at 7:30 on
a Saturday morning. I continue to be amazed by this tradition,
now almost three decades long, and we on campus are honored
by the dedication to Elmhurst College that all of you have shown
by just being here.

There are, of course, many reasons why someone might want
to visit a college campus (though perhaps at a more civilized
hour). Some colleges are beautiful places that provide a pleasant
backdrop for a casual stroll. Some have a lot of interesting activities, so they are great places to enjoy an exciting basketball game
or hear excellent musicians perform. Some are purposely small
colleges that focus on human interaction, always putting people
together so they can learn from each other. And some colleges
are places where there's a lot of good talk and dialogue going on
and where friends from outside the college are invited into the
discussion. Elmhurst is all of these things, but I hope that at least
one reason you visit the campus has to do with all that talking. I
hope you visit us in part to enter into, and enjoy, and learn from
the conversation that takes place here.

Talking is, in fact, one of the defining characteristics of a
good learning environment. Professors, in particular, have long
been identified with talking. One classic definition of a professor

is someone who talks in other people's sleep. But one of the things that modern learning theory has clearly established is something that old professor Socrates well understood—that is, that students learn best when *they* talk as well, when, in fact, they are in conversation—with each other and with a dedicated teacher. So in a sense, when we accept an applicant, we are saying to that student, "Let's talk."

But for something so natural and so human, talking with each other turns out to be a rather complicated thing. Somewhere far back in the shadows of prehistory, an early *Homo sapiens* greeted her companion, invited him into her cave, and said for the very first time in their rudimentary language, "Let's talk." Well, somewhere in the past someone said that for the first time, and I think that is the moment when human civilization began. To be sure, there would have been plenty of communication before this happened—shouted warnings, cheers for the successful hunt, arguments over territory. But suddenly, in that simple sentence this ancient ancestor stepped outside of just saying words and thought about talking. The discovery of this God-given ability to think about talking set this emerging human being apart from other animals.

Many, many years later, people who called themselves philosophers would still be thinking about talking. For Socrates in ancient Greece, conversation was the noblest thing people could do. It was the method by which humankind might—together—discover virtue and truth, which they could never find on their own. And when those early Greek teachers wanted to create the perfect and quintessentially human moment, they would invite a group of interesting people to a symposium—a dinner party where host and guests shared a pleasant meal as a backdrop to their intellectual conversation. The word *symposium* meant—quite literally—drinking together, but it was well understood that the food and drink were a metaphor for the more important nourishment of the mind that was the real reason for the event.

We at Elmhurst College have many dreams for our future. One of the most important is that we increasingly become, in the eyes of our students and for all those who surround us in the community, a place where there is always a rich conversation going on. Our Action Plan uses the expression, "a vital intellectual and cultural center." One of our good friends put it more poetically the other day when she used the phrase, "a spa for the mind."

That is our dream, and with some frequency that is our reality. You have before you a list of lectures and guest speakers we have provided for the community over the course of just the current academic year. The point of the list is to illustrate one kind of talk that takes place here. Our aim is not so much celebrity status as content, and we want to provide a nourishing feast for the mind. And that is why I hope no one ever comes on campus to share a meal with us—even an early Saturday morning breakfast—without experiencing in some small way why we like to say that Elmhurst is what college ought to be.

But that being said, there is still a big challenge in that simple phrase, "let's talk." In fact, I would say that our inability in today's society to say that often enough and to do it well enough is one of the serious problems of our era. Part of the difficulty is that there are a lot of terrible models out there, and lots of people seem to think that following those models is what talking is all about. Certainly among the worst are some of the so-called talk shows and the junk talk that is proliferating so rapidly on the Internet.

But consider the following more benign and everyday scenario: You are the chair of the program committee for your favorite organization, and you decide to propose the idea of having a program on the local issue *du jour*—a controversy that has begun to polarize the community. What are the ideas you are likely to hear from your committee? Well, one of the first may be that it is too controversial so the organization shouldn't get involved. But soon thereafter will come the classic, almost instinctive, approach. Someone will suggest that you invite two speakers, representatives of the two sides of the issue. Give them both a chance to speak and you can call it a debate, and that will ensure that the members of the audience on both sides of the issue will feel represented. If the two advocates are spirited enough and maybe make a few extreme statements, you may get especially good press coverage, and the organization will feel good about contributing to the community.

What's wrong with this picture? Well, consider the assumptions that are embedded in that plan. To take the most obvious, there is the assumption that there are two and only two sides to the issue. And why assume "sides" at all? This is clearly the terminology of games or battles. How might the model change if we referred instead to the various "facets" of an issue or problem? The reference here would be to the different ways a jewel reflects light when seen from different angles.

And why assume that the best way to examine a problem is to get spokespersons for the extreme ends of the spectrum of opinions to advocate their views? Might there be a role for someone who could explain the different perspectives fairly and in their most persuasive form and then analyze why the differences have occurred and how some fresh insight might help people in the community move closer together rather than continue toward increased polarization? There is a speaker series in downtown Chicago that has purposely tried to move away from the model of two talking heads advocating contrasting positions. Here is how the series is described: "The Michigan Avenue Forum provides a platform for individuals who can shed light on complex problems that plague Chicago, the nation and the world." Shedding light on complex problems sounds like very helpful talk indeed.

My point is simply that how we talk about our talking and how we think about it makes a difference, and that the little phrase "let's talk" involves a lot of important choices. Back in 1960, a mathematician by the name of Anatol Rapoport wrote a book that had wide influence at the time in the emerging field of game theory. It was an attempt to bring scientific insight to human conflict, from personal relations to international relations. He called it *Fights, Games, and Debates*. Some conflicts, he said, have the characteristics of a dogfight—a glare leads to a glare in response and then a snarl, which leads to a snarl in response and then a swipe. Soon the whole thing has degenerated into a brawl until one dog is either physically overcome or gives up and runs away. A fight is an encounter that goes downhill as inescapably as a ski slope. The opponent becomes an enemy to be eliminated.

Other conflicts, Rapoport says, are somewhat different. Consider an athletic event, for example. No matter how intense the rivalry, the contest depends on a good deal of cooperation. We agree to a time and place, to play a particular game with certain rules, and we agree to a set of controls that keep the conflict from turning into a fight. Typically, the objective is to score points that are positive to one side and negative to the other, and one side wins by rational strategy rather than by simply overpowering in the non-rational logic of the fight.

The third type of conflict, the debate, has the objective of convincing an opponent to change his or her mind—at least in principle. Of course, many exchanges we call debates are really games, and we speak, significantly, of "making points." But what

Rapoport calls a debate is a conflict whose purpose is not to eliminate another, and not to gain some advantage, but rather to persuade the other of one's own position.

Obviously, we can use Rapoport's typology to characterize the conversations we hear or that we undertake ourselves. We have certainly witnessed and probably participated in verbal "fights," where the discussion went downhill almost by itself. The next step up from this low form of talk is the conversation that is a game, where we exercise some level of civility, but are basically after scoring points. You've certainly heard this sort of talking, and very likely you've experienced the pleasure of exercising your wit in an exchange where repartee is the main point. A good game may be fun to watch, but it may not be exactly what we have in mind when we say, "let's talk."

In a conversation that is a debate, the point is to get your opponent to think again and possibly be won over to your position. As we've seen with our example from a community organization, debates are often staged more for the purpose of getting observers or members of the audience to think about the positions taken. This is not a bad framework for conversation, but obviously there's a big risk that such a dialogue might slip into really being merely a game or even a fight. Some years ago a Russian visitor by the name of Boris Marshalov sat in on a debate in a session of Congress and was later asked to describe what he observed. "Congress is so strange," Marshalov said. "A man gets up to speak and says nothing. Nobody listens—and then everybody disagrees." One reason people often turn away from the normal discourse of party politics is that they listen expecting to hear at least a debate but quickly conclude that it's only a game.

Rapoport's typology of fights, games, and debates is a helpful way to categorize the conversations that fill our experience, and we might try, when we have some influence, to nudge some of those conversations up to a higher model. But I want to suggest that by focusing on the conflicts of human interaction, Rapoport has missed a model that should be even closer to our hearts as people committed to learning. Remember the image of truth as a many-faceted gem? What if we began a conversation without starting by taking a side? What if the purpose of our conversation were really to try to understand something we don't understand or to learn something about a friend's thinking that doesn't seem to fit our stereotype? What if our objective were not to prove a point but to improve a situation?

I would suggest that there is a fourth model—what we might call deliberation. The dictionary defines *deliberation* as the consideration and discussion of alternatives *before* reaching a decision. The Latin root is *librare*, to weigh—remember the constellation Libra, the scales?

Conversation as deliberation is talking in order to weigh ideas, to improve our thinking, not just to display it. People talk differently when they are deliberating. They ask questions, they try on possible conclusions to test them, but without becoming committed to them. And while in this mode of conversation, people tend to listen differently as well. We listen not to protect ourselves as in a fight, or to get clues about our opponent's strategies as in a game, or to see if our position has been demolished as in a debate. In deliberative conversation we seek out people who think differently and we listen because the other person in the dialogue has something we might need—a better idea, or a new way of looking at things, or at least a better understanding of differences.

We may associate deliberation with something judges do with methodical seriousness, but in fact conversations that are deliberative may turn out to be quite energetic and even unruly. The key is the model the participants are holding in their minds. If you think you are in a fight or a game, you are. But if you are honestly interested in deliberating—and if you are lucky enough to find a partner who is similarly inclined—your conversation may be like a gentle and playful stream running through your time together, or it may be a stormy sea you ride together like sailors relishing the challenge. The purpose and promise of deliberation is better thinking, richer understanding of how different people might reach different conclusions, and a mind that is open, well exercised, and strong.

There are, of course, times when we must move beyond deliberation to judgment, when we must take a stand. But perhaps a clear grasp of the different forms of talk may help us develop the special skills of each and a sense of what type of talking is appropriate to what circumstances. To paraphrase our patron saint, we need the serenity to deliberate when we should be using the opportunity to learn, the courage to make judgments when we should move beyond deliberation, and the wisdom to know the difference.

The world in which we live—the world in which our graduates will live—is full of a lot of very problematic talk. As a nation we've endured month after month in the dark night of a multilayered tragedy with no heroes, but an incredible amount of talk. If there is anything we need now, it is a spirit of deliberation, the spirit of thinking together about the future rather than fighting about it, the spirit of listening to others to learn how so many reasonable people could be thinking so differently, the spirit of allowing ourselves to learn and grow, both individually and as a society.

We in this room are people who value education and who know what it means to love a college where people can grow into thinking, engaged professionals and citizens. We who have this connection have a special opportunity and a special challenge. The short form of that challenge is "let's talk." Let's find ways, in our daily lives and work, to model what it can mean to really talk with each other. Let's measure the talk that surrounds us against a high standard and recognize the enormous quantity of fights and games masquerading as useful talk. And let's continue our commitment to, and our support for, this college as a place devoted to the spirit of deliberation. So as we go into the chores and the pleasures of this day and into the weeks and months ahead, let's talk—let's really talk.

Thank you for coming to this morning's symposium, thank you for all you do for Elmhurst College and for our community, and thank you for all the ways you touch the world around you to help make it a better place.

TWENTY-FOUR

Solvitur Ambulando—
It Is Solved By Walking

THE PRESIDENT'S HOLIDAY DINNER
DECEMBER 2, 2007

The Greek philosopher Zeno, who lived around 450 B.C., loved to demonstrate the power of logic. His favorite device was to pose what he called a "paradox" in order to prove that what we think we see in everyday terms is in fact logically impossible. Consider this simple example: I set out to walk from here to there. But before I can get there, I must first cover half of the distance. But I am unable to travel that distance until I have first moved half that far. Continue this infinitely, and you will see that I really cannot go any distance at all, because before I do so, I must do something else, namely, cover half that distance. And therefore any motion is logically impossible.

Generations of philosophy students have struggled to solve this puzzle, but at some point some Latin scholar provided the simplest possible answer: *solvitur ambulando,* or "it is solved by walking." The way to cut through the maze of speculation is by straightforward experiment.

We really don't know who coined the phrase; one tradition is that it was Saint Augustine. But in any case, it is a classically simple strategy. In the late nineteenth century, Lewis Carroll, the Oxford philosopher who wrote *Alice in Wonderland* in his free time, published an essay that borrowed another of Zeno's paradoxes, this one proving that even the great warrior Achilles could not possibly outrun the slow and deliberate Tortoise—if the Tortoise were given a head start—since during whatever time it took Achilles to catch up to the Tortoise, the latter had moved some distance further ahead. And when Achilles reached that point, the Tortoise had in that time moved a bit further—over and over again in an infinite series but always leaving some remaining distance. In Carroll's version, the dialogue opens with Achilles not only having overtaken the Tortoise, but comfortably seated on its back.

> "So," [said the Tortoise,] "you've got to the end of our race-course?...
> Even though it DOES consist of an infinite series of distances? I
> thought some wiseacre or other had proved that the thing couldn't
> be done?" "It CAN be done," said Achilles. "It HAS been done!
> *Solvitur ambulando.*"

I don't know what role walking has played in your life, but my guess is that most of us in this room can recall something that happened while we were walking that for some reason is etched in the recesses of our mind. Some examples from my own memory bank that may trigger your own recollections: a walk home from elementary school late on a cold winter evening carrying my violin and a load of books (I have no idea why I remember that so distinctly, but I do); a long walk on a stunning summer night while on sentry duty at Parris Island; two walks down an aisle, one with Jeanette, the other with our daughter Sarah; a late-night walk through the bustling streets of Cairo with our other daughter, Elizabeth; and many, many long walks thinking through the crisis *du jour* during three decades of college administration. What are the walks that have stuck in your memory?

Walking is a quintessential human experience that is profoundly linked to learning. When our distant ancestors developed the knack of upright locomotion, their hands were freed to craft the tools whose use stretched their minds. Fast-forward a million and a half years or so to the ancient Greeks, and we find walking at the core of teaching and learning in the very first colleges. Plato started his little school by taking regular walks with his students in a park on the outskirts of Athens, an old olive grove named the Hekademia after the legendary hero Akademos. Soon these walks became a tradition—students took to calling it the Academy—with teacher and students organizing their curriculum around morning and afternoon walks.

Plato's prize student, Aristotle, went on to create his own school near the shrine of Apollo Lyceus. The campus consisted simply of some covered walkways where Aristotle strolled each day with his students, but this school came to be called the Lyceum and produced a group of brilliant scholars widely known as the "peripatetic" philosophers—literally, those who walked about. And so at the heart of the Western tradition of higher education and of every great college experience is a walk with a teacher.

My hope for the future of Elmhurst College is that it will always have at its heart the spirit of a walk with a teacher. A good college like Elmhurst is more peripatetic than might appear on the surface. In a world that honors speed and efficiency, the discipline of a liberal arts education is a different sort of journey. It demands that students slow down, think through some of the big questions of life, and take the time to observe nature and the human experience for themselves. It assumes direct and close human interaction where professors share themselves as people, not just as subject-matter experts. It requires the space to explore, to hone one's curiosity and creativity, even to venture down a blind alley or two—the last thing the world needs is people who have never learned how to learn from their mistakes. In a culture that is increasingly obsessed with virtual reality and simulated experiences, a fine small college is the real thing.

A walk with a teacher may take many different forms. In our age, students need to leave the groves of Hekademia and walk into the city and into other lands to experience, to observe, and to reflect upon the varieties of the human condition. A good internship or mentorship or clinical experience offers a chance to walk beside a professional and feel firsthand the pulse of the work that the textbook has only described. Without a global perspective, our graduates will be poorly prepared for professional or personal life in the coming years, and they need international opportunities to walk with people who are very different and to get a personal feel for our ultimate interdependence. And we will want to model the adaptation of new technology to enhance rather than undermine our students' ability to walk with many teachers.

Ultimately, the work that you, the friends of Elmhurst College, are supporting is the preparation of the next generation for the many different walks of their lives. As lifelong learners ourselves, we know a thing or two about these varied walks, and we owe it to ourselves and to those whose lives we touch to pay attention to doing them well.

First, there is the walk of thinking. A walk with a teacher is certainly one example, but there are so many ways to engage the mind by walking. The strolling lessons of Plato and Aristotle were not really new. Walking has been understood as an aid to thought and meditation for a very long time. Religious and educational architecture has through the centuries given special attention to the connection. The covered walkways of ancient cloisters sheltered monks and scholars as they paced in prayer or deep in thought. The mysterious labyrinths in the floors of medieval cathedrals have inspired meditative walking for centuries. All of us who are inclined to walk when we are trying to concentrate can understand what Jean Jacques Rousseau was getting at when he wrote in his *Confessions*, "I can only meditate when I am walking. When I stop, I cease to think; my mind works only with my legs."

Then there is the walk of pilgrimage. Sometimes we walk because there is some very special objective. This sort of walk, too, is deeply embedded in our essential humanity. It is recognizable in most religious traditions, from the sacred journey to Jerusalem, to the Hajj of the devout Muslim, to the pilgrims of the Middle Ages walking reverently—sometimes on their knees—to holy sites. Many of the struggles of our lives can best be understood as pilgrimages—some big goal out there in the distance, long and sustained effort to get there, fighting fatigue to put one foot in front of the other, and finally, if we are lucky, a sense of having arrived. The wise person chooses worthy goals, but just as important, learns to value the journey for its own sake.

Just as central to our humanity is the walk of companionship. "Let's go for a walk together" is a simple and beautiful gift. In some strange way our parallel steps help to align our thoughts as well, and we discover each other in fresh ways. It is just the sort of attitude and relationship that effective partnership and teamwork require. How much better the world might be if more people stepped across boundaries to take a walk with a stranger. How much better our lives would be if we walked toward, rather than away from, those closest to us. As the old proverb reminds us: "A real friend is one who walks in when the rest of the world walks out."

For most of us, the walk of faith is the journey of a lifetime. Step by step, experience by experience, we seek, we listen. There are times when it is a walk through the valley of the shadow, and there are times when we sense more clearly the mystery and the miracle in which we are embedded. The Vietnamese Buddhist monk Thich Nhat Hanh put it this way:

> People usually consider walking on water or in thin air a miracle. But I think the real miracle is not to walk either on water or in thin air, but to walk on earth. Every day we are engaged in a miracle which we don't even recognize: a blue sky, white clouds, green leaves, the black, curious eyes of a child—our own two eyes. All is a miracle.

The walk of faith is a journey into and through that miracle and on toward living faithfully.

Finally, there is the walk for which we hope our students will be ready when their moment comes—the walk of courage. There are times when something needs to be said, when a burden needs to be shared, when where we walk tells who we are. The scholarly Rabbi Abraham Joshua Heschel found himself at such a moment in 1965 when he chose to join a southern Black preacher on a walk from Selma to Montgomery. Afterward, he wrote, "For many of us the march...was about protest and prayer. Legs are not lips and walking is not kneeling. And yet our legs uttered songs. Even without words, our march was worship. I felt my legs were praying."

These are some of the walks of life for which Elmhurst College is preparing its graduates—the walk of thinking and learning, the walk of pilgrimage and accomplishment, the walk of companionship and engagement, the walk of faith, and the walk of courage. We are immensely grateful for the friendship and support of everyone gathered here tonight—friendship and support that in so many ways has enabled our college to become better and better at preparing our students for the walks of their lives.

As we enter this joyous and holy time of year, I hope that

each of you will find time to take a walk. Take a walk to clear your mind and think. Make a pilgrimage—even a short one—to some place that matters to you. Take a walk of companionship with someone you love and perhaps with someone you don't know at all. Take a few more steps on your walk of faith by reflecting on the gifts that mean the most. And be alert to those moments when you have a chance to walk with courage into a world that needs what you can offer.

St. Augustine, the early church father from North Africa, had a wonderful way of using everyday experiences to inspire his readers. In one of his sermons, he calls on us to press on with the journey of life and learning. "Always be dissatisfied with what you are," he writes, "if you want to arrive at what you are not yet. Because wherever you are satisfied with yourself, there you are stuck. Always add some more. Always keep on walking. Always forge ahead!"

The world in which we find ourselves is confusing. Our lives are complicated. Sometimes it seems that Zeno may have had a point about the impossibility of moving forward. But in the end, simple things—simple, everyday, human things—can cut through the fog of complexity and the noise of competing ideologies. Sometimes, at least, it may be as simple as walking. *Solvitur ambulando.* So the message I hope you will carry with you into this cold night and into the warmth of the wonderful season ahead—with its long list of all the things you need to do—is the reminder given us by the prophet Micah—that life is simpler than it may seem. All that is truly required of you is "to do justice, and to love kindness, and to *walk*—humbly—with your God."

VII *Endings*

Mind the Gap

COMMENCEMENT ADDRESS
FEBRUARY 10, 2002

E very family develops over time a special language. Shared experience leads to a shared dialect, as we use words and phrases to remind each other of the moments and relationships that make up our unique saga. Let me share an example from the Cureton family.

When our older daughter, Elizabeth, was in junior high school, she and I traveled one summer in France and England. We had an especially fine time in London, where we were part of the cheering crowd at a royal wedding. Alas, the marriage did not turn out as well as our trip. But even today, she or I can say three little words to each other, and we are back at Buckingham Palace or Trafalgar Square. Anyone who has ridden on the London Underground will already have recognized those three words in the title of these remarks.

The subway system in London was built before modern building codes, and there is one design quirk about which you have to be careful. There are a lot of curves in the tracks and many Underground stations are on these curves. As a consequence, there is often a considerable space between the platform and the subway car into which you are stepping. To remind you to pay attention so that you don't end up stepping into the void, a voice over a loudspeaker repeats—over and over—"Mind the gap; mind the gap."

Somehow that very British way of saying "watch your step"
became as much a souvenir of our trip as our photographs, and
for years Elizabeth and I have had a special way to say good-bye
or to wish each other good luck. Three little words, recycled from
a mundane safety warning in a foreign city and transformed into
a private code for affection and concern—*Mind the Gap.*

So I want to say to this graduating class in the winter of 2002:
Mind the Gap. Other phrases like "congratulations" and "good
luck" are perfectly appropriate, too, but I want to add a special
word of encouragement about some of the gaps—some of the
special challenges—that lie ahead of you. Each of you took a big
step when you entered Elmhurst and began your studies here.
Now you are taking another big step as you complete this phase
of your education and move forward to new challenges. A good
general rule in life is: When you're taking big steps, pay attention
to what you're doing.

The story is told of the days when General Francisco Franco,
the Spanish dictator, would give occasional radio addresses to the
Spanish people. During one of these, he spoke of the great diffi-
culties facing the nation as its economy was disintegrating. "You
need to know," he told his listeners, "that the prospects are not
good; we stand at the edge of a great chasm; an enormous abyss
lies ahead of us." The next week Franco was on the air again, this
time to announce some stern governmental measures to address
the problems. "Men and women of Spain," he began, "last week
I told you that we faced a great chasm, an enormous abyss. I am
pleased to report that the government has acted. We have taken
a bold step forward."

The gaps I want to think about with you for a few minutes
are more subtle. And they are not simply spaces to be stepped over
in single steps—even big steps. They are matters you will wrestle

with for the rest of your lives. One such gap has to do with the difference between what you have and who you are. Here is how psychologist Erich Fromm, echoing the early Christian thinker St. Augustine, makes the distinction: "Two verbs have built two empires, the verb 'to have' and the verb 'to be.' The first is the empire of things—material possessions and power. The second is an empire of spirit—things that last."

I recall once hearing a very successful young lawyer speaking to a college class about his career. He hoped, he said, to give them some advice that would help them be as successful as he had been. When he invited questions, one student asked him how he balanced the demands of family and profession. Well, the lawyer said, he really didn't have that problem because, unlike many of his colleagues, he had never married and had no family. He said that occasionally he would wonder if he was missing something, but he never let it get him down. His therapy, he said, was to go to his garage and spend a little time polishing his Porsche, and he went on to describe how much he enjoyed driving a very expensive car. I found myself hoping that the students in the class were smart enough to understand how sad that story was.

Learning how to live in a materialistic society but at the same time to rise above it to become a person who nurtures the relationships of family and friends, who contributes to the lives of others, who helps to build better communities, who values the life of the mind and the life of the spirit—that requires bridging the huge gap between the world of things and money and the world of people and values. For many of us, the insights of our faith communities provide guidance as we negotiate this difficult space. One of the silver linings of the dark days of September 2001 may have been a cultural shift toward greater attention to things that matter in the long run. There is clear evidence of a lot of people reconsidering aspects of their personal lives. What is less clear is whether it will last. In any case, each of us will face for the rest of our lives that distance between having and being. Mind the gap.

Next, I hope you will pay attention to the giant leap between getting a job and becoming a true professional. Most of you in this class already know what it means to hold a job, although you may not have achieved *the* job, the one to which you aspire. And many of you have found here at Elmhurst College much that will help you get and keep that job that you want. But I hope you have found something much bigger here. This is a liberal arts college, where all students explore a range of different ways of knowing and get used to thinking critically and creatively. For us, liberal learning is not an abstract exercise divorced from real life. We recognize that your career as a professional will be a major part of how you will live as a liberally educated person. And we hope you will bring the full depth of your mind and your heart to the work you will do in the world.

That work will require skill and competence, of course; any job does. But what the world needs are true professionals who apply their expertise with integrity and with thoughtful attention to the impact of what they are doing. When we see around us the trail of broken promises and diminished lives left by those who did their jobs with more cleverness than judgment, we appreciate anew what it means to bring the highest standards of professionalism to whatever work we do. You will all have jobs; my wish for you is that you will go far beyond that and become true professionals. Mind the gap between the two.

And finally, there is a gap I hope you see more clearly now than when you began your college studies. It is the space between what you know and what there is yet to be known. In a sense, this gap is what higher education is all about. On the surface, it may seem a bit ironic that at a college dedicated to spreading knowledge, we seem always to be resisting knowledge. We challenge assumptions, we try to disprove hypotheses, and we emphasize the limitations of what we know. But the underlying principle here is critically important. Accepting the incompleteness and tentativeness of what we know is essential to keeping our minds alive and inquiring and growing.

This openness to new answers and better questions does not mean we need to stop making decisions because we can never know enough. Indeed, learning to act in conditions of uncertainty and to take risks when we should is part of coming to terms with the ever-continuing search for truth. Dealing with that space between our current understanding and what we would know if we had complete divine wisdom requires a balancing of intellectual humility with the courage to continue to inquire and study and learn.

We live in an era full of sharp reminders of the evil that can result from the illusion of absolute knowledge held absolutely. When education becomes closed, blind indoctrination, the search for truth comes to an end and the rest of us are at risk. We continue to ask questions, to listen carefully to divergent voices, and to test knowledge in the crucible of debate not just because we enjoy the challenge but because it is essential to our humanity. The words of T. S. Eliot deserve to be emblazoned on a banner over our campus: "There is more to understand. Hold fast to that as the way to freedom." So mind the gap between what you know now and what you will learn as you continue your lifelong search for better understanding. Value that gap, even as you work to make it ever smaller.

I believe that much of who you will become will be defined

by how you deal with these three gaps—how you wrestle with the space between trying to have and trying to be, how you work your way through the space between getting a job and becoming a true professional, and how you deal with what you don't know—that space filled with new insights and better understanding that is waiting for curious and courageous minds.

These gaps, then, are not emptiness to be stepped over and avoided. They are spaces where your creativity can have free reign. When the great pianist Arthur Schnabel was asked the secret of his playing, he replied, "The notes I handle no better than many other pianists. But the pauses between the notes—ah, that's where the art resides." It is, indeed, in the gaps that the art of living is exercised and polished.

The steps you take across this platform and down these stairs symbolize the completion of something significant. You are stepping off the platform of this stage of your formal education onto the moving train of the rest of your life. Step carefully, and you should have little difficulty negotiating the transition. But there are bigger challenges and opportunities ahead. There are spaces for you to fill with your unique gifts, your integrity, your energy, your enthusiasm for life and learning, and your commitment to making a difference in the world. Congratulations, and mind the gap!

TWENTY-SIX

Here There Be Dragons

COMMENCEMENT ADDRESS
FEBRUARY 6, 2005

O ne of the most prized artifacts in the collection of the New York Public Library is a small sphere called the Lenox Globe. It is about five inches in diameter, made of copper, and engraved on the surface are the continents and oceans of the world. That is, of course, the continents and oceans that were known when the globe was made, which scholars believe was in the early 1500s. The vague shape of the east coast of South America is labeled *Mundus Novus*—New World. Where we expect to see North America, the globe shows only a group of islands, one of which is labeled *Zipangri*—Japan.

As the earliest globe to reflect the discoveries of Columbus, the Lenox Globe is an immensely important piece of history. But it is also famous for a particularly intriguing inscription that appears on the east coast of what seems to be China. The Latin reads *Hic sunt Dracones*—here there are dragons. Scholars have debated just what this refers to, but there is no question how the unknown engraver of the Lenox Globe felt about the dangers of exploration; a variety of sea monsters and drawings of shipwrecks fill the oceans around his miniature world.

The early mapmakers of the European Age of Discovery worked on the leading edge of knowledge. As courageous sailors ventured away from familiar shores, they brought back bits of information—a stretch of coastline here, a strange island there.

But always there was that space on the charts about which nothing was yet known, the world beyond the familiar boundaries. How natural—how human—to fill the empty space with drawings of fearsome sea serpents and dragons that conveyed a not-so-subtle warning: "No one really knows what's here. Be afraid; be very afraid. *Hic sunt dracones.*"

Now at this point you may be thinking that my message to you graduates is that you are about to enter that space of dragons and monsters as you leave the known world of classrooms and textbooks, and that you need not worry because dragons are, after all, only mythical. Well, that's a good message as far as it goes, but in this final and very brief class session before you complete your studies at Elmhurst, I want to dig just a little deeper. Because, in a profound sense, all of us are mapmakers, and the choices you make about the spaces beyond the world as you know it will help shape your lives and influence how you manage the journeys ahead.

The world in which we live—and to which you are now poised to contribute in some special way—is more like the world depicted on the Lenox Globe than we might assume. There are parts that are familiar to us—our personal mental homelands in which each of us has been raised—what we today might call our comfort zones. But beyond these familiar lands lie the strange and the unknown. And the dragons that seem to be roaming out there are fearsome indeed.

I hope your years of formal education and particularly your Elmhurst years have helped prepare you for dealing with these dragons. First of all, I hope you are better able to recognize and overcome the dragons of aggressive ignorance. These are the forces unleashed when people insist on not learning, because they are either unaware of their ignorance or convinced they have already achieved complete truth.

The first challenge as you face such dragons is to recognize the limits of your own understanding. As you have been studying particular subjects, you have been honing that ability to assess what you know and how you know it. As you have been practicing the business of clarifying questions, testing assumptions, and examining evidence, you have been developing the capacity to know what you don't know. It may seem counterintuitive to think of learning, in large part, as discovering what you don't know, but this principle runs through the long history of human inquiry. In 412 B.C., the Greek playwright Euripides wrote, "Man's most valuable trait is a judicious sense of what not to believe." David Gross, the physicist who won a Nobel Prize in 2004, puts it this way: "The most important product of knowledge is ignorance."

The ignorance of ignorance is a special threat when people conclude they don't need or want to know. An example is the lack of interest among so many Americans in the study of science, which leaves our polity ill equipped to consider important questions of public policy and especially susceptible to pseudoscientific nonsense. Refusing to take history seriously is just as dangerous. As historian Daniel Boorstin once put it, "Planning for the future without some sense of history is like planting cut flowers."

So I hope that in addition to a lot of knowledge, you will take with you a keen sense of the vastness of the unknown and a certain skepticism about the claims of those who believe they have found final truth. This is not a trivial matter. Aggressive ignorance is the enemy of a free society, and our future as a vibrant, dynamic people depends absolutely on keeping the windows of inquiry wide open. As T. S. Eliot reminds us in the words that are engraved on the fountain in Alumni Circle, "There is more to understand: hold fast to that as the way to freedom."

There is another species of dragons out there, and they populate the boundaries between *we* and *they*. These are the dragons of parochialism. Again, while here at Elmhurst you have been preparing for them. As you have been reading and learning about people in other cultures, living in different places or times, you have been broadening your definition of humanity. As you have been arguing in class with people whose views you don't understand, you have been preparing to be builders of bridges. If you have been lucky enough to have had some direct experience in a part of the world far from your home, you have taken a big step in the long journey toward a fuller understanding of just who you are.

But the dragons of parochialism are subtle and devious. They can turn the comfort we feel in familiar surroundings into fear of venturing forth. They can leave us blinded by tribal pride to what we might learn from others. They can turn patriotism into chauvinism. In short, by keeping us from learning of others, they keep us from fully knowing ourselves. Even during the height of British imperialism, Rudyard Kipling could see the risks when he wrote in 1891, "And what should they know of England who only England know?"

The dragons at the edges of the old maps remind us that we don't, in fact, know everything, and that different people and cultures and perspectives have much to teach us. But there is one final lesson in that ancient Latin warning, *Hic sunt dracones*. If the world outside our little village is important to us, it must be part of our ethics as well as our understanding. And here we come face-to-face with the dragons that Elmhurst's own Reinhold Niebuhr fought so vigorously—the dragons of self-centeredness and self-righteousness.

Perhaps more than anything else, we hope you will leave our college with a wider sense of responsibility and a deeper commitment to look beyond your own selfish interests. You have been working at this as you have studied how societies succeed or fail, explored the thinking of some of the great minds of the past, and reached out to others in service-learning projects and leadership in campus activities. One of the real strengths of Elmhurst is the range of ways you have prepared yourselves to be professionals in the highest sense of the term, pursuing excellence in your life's work in ways that make the world a better place.

But the dragons of self-centeredness and self-righteousness are particularly sneaky. They will tell you that personal integrity and commitment to your family and friends and church and neighbors are challenge enough and there's not much you can do about things like poverty or public health or social justice or the earth's environment or the problems of far-away countries. So human lives are pulled down by complex systems but also by good people too focused on themselves to notice the impact of their choices.

The ancient globe that warned of dragons in the unknown reaches was still a globe—at the time, a revolutionary way to think of the connectedness of continents and oceans. And from that germ of an idea, humankind may yet build a global ethic of mutual responsibility for all God's children. The question for each of us is whether we will give in to the dragons of self-centeredness or fight back by seeking some small way to live out the huge truth of human interdependence. In the words of the poet Gwendolyn Brooks, "We are each other's harvest; we are each other's business; we are each other's magnitude and bond."

You have been a part of Elmhurst through your years here, and Elmhurst will always be a part of you. As you continue your journey, the good wishes of all who remain here go with you. Carry as well the weapons you will need when you encounter those dragons that roam beyond the boundaries of the world as you know it. Fight aggressive ignorance by continuing to learn and grow. Seek out those who seek the truth, and keep at arm's length those who are certain they have found it. Fight the dragons of parochialism by building bridges over the boundaries that divide people, making some friends from among those with different perspectives, and striving for a global perspective. And don't let the dragons of self-centeredness pull you off course from your exploration of a passage to a better world.

Yes, there are dragons out there, but today the odds shift just a bit, because now there are some more graduates of Elmhurst College out there as well. Good for you. Good for us. Good for the world. Congratulations!

Who's in Charge Here?

COMMENCEMENT ADDRESS
FEBRUARY 6, 2000

I t is a special disease of students and teachers of political science to be intensely curious about patterns of influence. Invite those of us with this peculiar affliction into an office or a meeting room—or indeed any place where there are people—and we will immediately start wondering, Who's in charge here? Who is making things happen and who is keeping things from happening?

You may not share a particular interest in this specialized form of people watching. But I am reasonably certain that as you move into new opportunities or undertake new challenges now that you have finished college, you will need in one way or another to use that question in your daily life. You start a new job and you meet your boss and your fellow workers, and you immediately begin the process of trying to understand how the office or the company or the school or the hospital *really* works. You begin married life and discover right away that working out who is going to be in charge of what is an essential part of building the relationship.

Like the fundamental questions at the core of many of the disciplines you may have studied in college, this question will stick with you for a lifetime. The dynamics of the relationships among people are more than just endlessly fascinating. They drive how people get things done. And if *you* want to get things done—in your job, in your family, in your community—you will need to become adept at figuring out who's in charge and how you can use that understanding to help you do the good you want to do.

But I want to use these few minutes of the final short class before you receive your diploma and walk off into the sunset to remind you of a deeper purpose for this everyday question. When we ask this question about other people we are observing, it may lead to interesting and perhaps useful analysis. When we turn the question inward and ask it of ourselves, it becomes one of the most important challenges we face in life.

You may remember the story of the young fellow who brings his report card home from school. It's not a very good report card, and his parents let him know that very clearly and ask him what he thinks the problem is. "Well," says the little guy—who turns out to be pretty smart after all—"I can't decide what my real problem is. I can't decide whether it's heredity or environment."

As we enter adulthood, we steadily lose both of those excuses. But it is remarkable how we manage to cling to that schoolboy's theory and adapt it to fit new circumstances. Why did I get a B rather than an A in that course? Well, it wasn't at the most convenient time, and most days I was late because it took too long to find a parking place close by. The assignments weren't always clear to me, and with my job and other things I had to do, I sometimes couldn't keep up. And, of course, it was a rather boring subject, and the professor wasn't able to make it very exciting. How maddening it is to have a close friend or a parent or a professor listen to this litany and then say to us, "Okay, but why did you get a B?" Who's in charge here?

One of the great transformations of human history has been the gradual enlargement of the range of choices people have and the seemingly inexorable trend toward more individual decision making. We look back at earlier times through the lens of our own experience and see people limited by primitive technology, ground down by the need to struggle for mere existence, and constrained by political domination. In our era, however, we invent trains and automobiles and jet planes, and we increase the range of places we can be whenever we choose. We invent new means of communication so we can choose to know all kinds of things whenever we want to. We invent democratic politics and involve ourselves in choices our ancestors never could have imagined. And at the beginning of the third millennium of the Common Era, each of us, at least in our prosperous, Western circles, can enjoy comforts and make personal choices that would have been the envy of the richest kings of only a couple of centuries ago.

Or at least so it would seem. The practiced, critical eye of the graduate of a good liberal arts college will see just beneath the surface of this enormous freedom a paradox of individualism. The same technological forces that provide so much freedom and individual choice give us very powerful instructions as to what to choose and how to live. And so we see young people in less-developed countries all over the world expressing their newfound independence and individuality by coveting exactly the same jeans and popular music enjoyed by millions of young people all over the world. There are no more profound conformists than new freshmen arriving at college determined to express their individuality.

And now technology is ready to take this paradox to a new level as we move beyond choice to customization. The hundred channels on cable television turn out to be not the culmination of a trend but just the beginning. The new goal is to enable each of us to buy precisely what we want, configured just the way we want it, whenever we want it. In a very short time, each of us will be able to create the television channel of our dreams—all of what we like, all day. You like science fiction, very conservative politics, and country music? Fine, a few clicks and you can live in a virtual world in which you hear nothing else. Now it won't be some outside force that prevents you from seeing the whole world around you in all its diversity—that keeps you in your place, as it were—you will be able to do that for yourself, if you choose.

Who's in charge here? The overwhelming message of our era is that each person is king. The more subtle reality is that the choices available are not always what they seem, that commerce and culture are working very hard to manipulate those choices, that technology designed to liberate can also entrap, and that wide-ranging choice is very unevenly distributed in society. All that, of course, doesn't make things easier for us. In fact, it puts in our hands even more responsibility to make our choices wisely.

All this choosing can be overwhelming. And it goes far beyond just the arrangement of our everyday life. A few short generations ago, your life work would have been determined largely by your family circumstances, and you would likely end your life doing just what you had begun in late adolescence. Now we have so many choices that a college needs a special office to help you think them through, and we assume you will have several different careers in your working life, some in fields we cannot now imagine. The most important single fact for you to understand about your career is that from now on you are self-employed, and you must think about your career in those terms and assume personal responsibility for it.

Taking charge of our lives and assuming personal responsibility for the decisions that are ours are lifetime challenges. And we face these challenges wherever we find ourselves. A university president tells of his experience at a formal dinner on his campus, served by neatly dressed and well-trained student workers. When the young woman serving his table carefully placed two pats of butter on his bread plate, the president casually asked for some extra butter. "I'm sorry, sir," the student said, "I have clear instructions to put exactly two pats of butter on each bread plate." "You don't understand," the president said gently "I am President Smith, and I am in charge of this great university, and I would like some extra butter." "I am pleased to meet you, sir," the student replied. "My name is Susan, and *I* am in charge of the butter."

No matter how constrained our world may seem, personal choices, and therefore personal responsibility, always remain. At a far more serious level, Victor Frankl, the psychologist who survived the death camps of the Holocaust, writes in his book *Man's Search for Meaning* of the horrors of having everything stripped away and facing almost certain death. "There were always decisions to make," he writes:

> We who lived in concentration camps can remember the men who walked through the huts comforting others, giving away their last piece of bread. They may have been few in number, but they offer sufficient proof that everything can be taken away from a man but one thing: the last of the human freedoms—to choose one's attitude in any given set of circumstances, to choose one's own way.

We who find ourselves in such different circumstances, blessed by personal freedom and prosperity, informed by the insights of a good education, deluged with almost overwhelming possibilities, ultimately face exactly that challenge—to choose our own way. Those choices may be thoughtful and considered—or they may be made as though we had never bothered to get an education. They may be focused on benefiting others and doing something worthwhile in our communities and in the world—or they may be made with blind selfishness that in the long run destroys human society.

Who's in charge here? The diploma you are about to receive carries between its lines an answer to that question. The words say that you have achieved something important, that you have overcome obstacles to acquire a body of knowledge and experience. But think of it, as well, as a license to take charge of your own choices. Sometimes it may seem that you are only in charge of the butter. But the choices you make each hour of each day will define the person you have become. A college of character can hope for nothing more than that its graduates express their character in their lives, in their loves, and in their work. And so, from your alma mater comes this final, clear message: You are in charge. Congratulations!

The Memory Holes of the Wampanoag

COMMENCEMENT ADDRESS
FEBRUARY 4, 2007

In 1949, a novel appeared that was destined to make its way into classrooms across the English-speaking world and into the consciousness of an era. George Orwell's *1984* told a deeply disturbing story of a society that had been successfully undermined by Big Brother. Since then, high school students have written a mountain of essays wrestling with the story of Winston Smith, an employee of the Ministry of Truth, who tries to fight back, but ultimately fails.

As many of you will remember, Winston's job is to revise old editions of newspapers, changing their content to reflect what the Party now wants people to believe about the past. So if a government prediction published the previous year proved wildly inaccurate, the original publications were simply rounded up, new versions containing more convenient predictions were printed, and the old newspapers were eliminated. This last step was accomplished by depositing the embarrassing articles in slots placed around the office, openings known as "memory holes," which led down to hidden incinerators that left no trace of the old truth, which had now been, from the Party's perspective, "rectified." As Orwell writes, "Day by day and almost minute by minute the past was brought up to date."

And so was created a modern metaphor for the very old practice of perpetuating lies by willfully ignoring or even destroying contradictory evidence. The frightening future Orwell describes is based fundamentally on this ability to control a whole society by wiping out memory and thereby eliminating independent thinking. No tool in Big Brother's inventory was more sinister than the memory holes of the Ministry of Truth.

But Orwell's novel was intended as a warning that we should seek a different future. And, as so often happens, we can find clues about such a better future in the past. This year, America will be recalling a special part of its collective history, a part that began exactly four hundred years ago with the founding of the first permanent English settlement in Jamestown, Virginia, in 1607. A few years later, a small group of religious nonconformists—pilgrims seeking a place to live as they wished—arrived in Massachusetts. These two fragile footholds led to an encounter between what the settlers called the Old World and the New that would transform a continent and create a very new world indeed. The story of those difficult beginnings is a complex mix of courage and treachery, of nobility and tragedy. And hidden in the record of those early years is one small reference to some memory holes that could not have been more different from those of Orwell's *1984*.

One of the biggest needs of the first settlers was more settlers, who would bring with them more resources from the mother country. Several reports were sent back to England in the early 1600s to publicize the ventures and to drum up interest in new investments. One was titled *Good Newes from New England: a true Relation of things very remarkable at the Plantation of Plimoth in New England*. In it, one of the original pilgrims, Edward Winslow, tells of the journey on the *Mayflower*, the first encounters with the natives, and the struggles through hardship and dangers. One section includes Winslow's observations about the people the settlers called Indians. Winslow had spent a good deal of time with these strange men and women who called themselves the Wampanoag. He had visited their villages, and traveled with them for days at a time along the ancient pathways through the forest. It was no doubt on one of these journeys that he learned something about how the Indians remembered and taught their own history. The small holes he spotted from time to time along the trail turned out to have special meaning for his Wampanoag companions. Whenever they passed one, his guides would begin a story about something that had happened nearby, perhaps generations before. Here is Winslow's description, in the language of the 1620s:

> Instead of records and chronicles, they take this course. Where any remarkable act is done, in memory of it, either in the place, or by some pathway near adjoining, they make a round hole in the ground, about a foot deep, and as much over; which when others passing by behold, they inquire the cause and occasion of the same, which being once known, they are careful to acquaint all men, as occasion serveth, therewith; and lest such holes should be filled, or grown up by any accident, as men pass by, they will oft renew the same; by which means many things of great antiquity are fresh in memory. So that as a man traveleth, if he can understand his guide, his journey will be the less tedious, by reason of the many historical discourses [which] will be related unto him.

Just small holes by the side of the path. But imagine what those memory holes must have meant to people without a written language and with precious few tools with which to create monuments. What an elegant method of tapping into their well-honed skill of repeating the stories that made up their history and identity as a people. Simply dig out a small hole along the pathway as a reminder of an important event, and count on the powerful social bonds that united the tribe to assure that subsequent passersby would inquire, would retell, and would refresh the memory for the next travelers. And how startled the English settlers must have been as they traveled the pathways through the woods with their mysterious companions to discover that they were surrounded not by a dreary wilderness, but by a rich landscape of meaning. As Nathaniel Philbrick puts it in his book, *Mayflower*, "Winslow [and his colleagues] began to see that they were traversing a mythic land, where a sense of community extended far into the distant past."

The memory holes of the Wampanoag are long gone, victims of the decimation of the native tribes and the transformation of the physical environment as the European settlers swept across the land. But were those memory holes all that far from our own experience? A few years ago here at Elmhurst, I taught a seminar on the history of higher education in which one of the required readings was *An Ever Widening Circle*, the history of Elmhurst College. All those stories of Old Main and the College farm that became the Mall and the holes that were filled by faith, and the people behind the names of Irion and Niebuhr and Lehmann and the others—all these were windows into the larger saga of American colleges in general. At the end of the course, as we were all sharing our experiences, one student said that that book and the stories it tells had been the best part of the course. "Now," she said, "when I walk across campus, everything means something."

"Now everything means something." For that student, the things we pass by every day had become like the Indian memory holes. The names, the buildings, the spaces, had become reminders of stories that enriched the landscape and reminded her of her place here. I can imagine a time years from now when that woman brings her children to show them where she went to college. And

I can imagine those stories being retold, enhanced by the tales of what *she* did here and what it meant to her.

"Now everything means something." You who are the first wave of the Class of 2007 have come to the end of one stage in your lifelong journey on the pathway to becoming educated people. If we were to try to define in simple terms the ultimate objective—the goal of that long journey—I'm not sure we could improve on that brief statement. For the truly educated person, everything means something.

For the student who has studied literature, the poem that just won't go away has become so rich with meaning that it keeps on teaching. For someone who knows about sociology, a walk down a city street becomes a tapestry of patterns and questions. For the student of accounting, the dry numbers of an annual report are alive with implications. For someone who has spent time in a science laboratory, the natural world is a constant wonder of interactions and evolutions and the interplay of forces. And for the person educated in the liberal arts tradition, lots of things mean something, and the connections among them mean even more. In the end, learning is all about stories with meaning—the stories of our values, the stories of our understanding of how the world works, and the story of our own place in the world.

But there is another layer in the story of the Wampanoag memory holes. Yes, they served as reminders of the history that bound the tribe together. But that bond itself helped turn the memory holes into triggers of action. The hole by the pathway was not there simply to suggest private reflection. The message to the passing tribesman was: Get busy; there is a purpose to this knowledge. Share the stories, work together to seek and keep the truth, and refresh the memory hole so it serves the next traveler well. Thus the seemingly quiet reminder by the side of the trail carried with it a call to action, an obligation to be an engaged participant in the process of exploring and applying knowledge.

That's the way it is when everything means something. Knowledge is restless and wants to be put to some use. Learning about things that are wrong in the world nudges us toward doing something about it. Really getting to know people who are different from us is an invitation to build bridges of understanding. Digging deeper into our research increases rather than decreases the work yet to be done. The best answers raise even more interesting questions.

And so we are left with two kinds of memory holes—two different ways to think about how to learn and how to live. And every day we choose. There is the way of the memory holes of *1984*, throwing away the past and what we might learn from it, letting our decisions be made by ideology rather than by informed and creative thinking, and adjusting our principles to whatever seems convenient at the moment. It is the way to a life without meaning. Or there are the memory holes of the Wampanoag, the markers that remind us to remember, to seek the meaning that is below the surface, to reach back to deeper truths—and forward to how we will live out our commitments. Your years of education have been preparing you to notice the markers by the side of the path and to live lives that mean something.

This, then, is your alma mater's hope for each of you—that day by day the wilderness through which you travel will become more and more meaningful as your life fills with memory holes. And may the stories you learn and tell and live by enrich and enhance your life and the lives of all those you influence. Congratulations!

TWENTY-NINE

Wider Circles for Elmhurst College

FOUNDERS DAY ADDRESS
FEBRUARY 12, 2008

For hundreds of years, Polynesian sailors crisscrossed the vast Pacific Ocean, spreading their influence throughout the widely separated islands. The most important person on their simple outrigger canoes was the "wayfinder" who set the course, monitored progress, and pointed the vessels toward their destinations. On the ponderous sailing ships of European explorers, the navigator would bring along his charts and compass and sextant and, eventually, an accurate chronometer. The Polynesian wayfinder had none of these instruments; his tools were simply his eyes, his ears—and his memory.

Becoming a good wayfinder was the work of a lifetime. He needed to know the stars and their movements, the sun and its subtle messages at sunrise and sunset. He needed to be able to read the sea and understand what the birds overhead might tell him. But very importantly, he needed to remember where he had come from. As he set out on a voyage, the wayfinder would look back and align the canoe with two or three particular landmarks on shore in order to set a course. From then on, every change of course and everything affecting the canoe—wind, temperature, the movement of the swells and how the sea *felt*—everything would become part of the mental record. Whenever he needed to, the wayfinder could retrace it all in his mind, reconstruct each adjustment, and know in which direction home lay and how far away it was. His mental maps and the stars helped him imagine his destination, but he always knew where he was because he could look back in his mind's eye and point to home.

Our modern minds are less sophisticated and our tools are more clever, but in the long run we too must learn to remember where we have come from if we are to move confidently toward the future. And that is why we are here, celebrating Founders Day. It is one small way, even if mostly symbolic, to turn around and look back at the receding landmarks by which we might align—or alter—our course. I want to take a moment today to point out three of them—three points of reference from our legacy. Each is something worth remembering, and each offers a lens through which we might look ahead.

First is the special heritage of Elmhurst College as an international transplant. The fourteen young men who arrived at the train station in 1871 along with their professor, Inspektor Kranz, were very much strangers in a strange land. Most had been born in Germany; all spoke primarily German, as their school would do for decades. Much of the early history of Elmhurst centered on the struggle to reconcile the hope of maintaining their German culture in their new land with the need to address the reality of their American context.

When the young President H. Richard Niebuhr wrote to the graduating class of 1925 in their yearbook, he could point with some pride to the school's first graduates to complete a true four-year baccalaureate degree in the American fashion. He knew that moving beyond the German *gymnasium* model that his father's generation had brought with them was a necessary and positive step. But he did not dismiss that distinctive heritage; he reframed it. Even as Elmhurst became a more American college, it still, Niebuhr argued, had something unique to offer America. As he wrote in *The Elms*, this special contribution "which Elmhurst College hopes to make to its students and through them to an ever-widening circle is the transmission of the best elements in that culture which its founders brought to America."

In other words, Niebuhr was suggesting, we need not abandon something that is at our core just because the outward structures and even the curricular framework is adapting to changing conditions. The distinctive German contributions in scholarship, the arts, and even religious thought might still resonate, even in an American college. Looking back, we can see that the essence of what Elmhurst had to offer was a more global perspective in comparison with other schools of its time.

We also know that a particular phrase in Niebuhr's comments stuck in the institution's consciousness, and "the ever-widening circle" has become a part of our lexicon and even the name of our history. The image gives us a way of interpreting both our development as a college and our growth as individual members of a community of learners. But at the center of that ever-widening circle of Elmhurst College was an international experience. What might it mean for a college of our time to look back and align our thinking with the fact that our founders traveled thousands of miles to come here to college and then hoped to contribute to international understanding? Taking that starting point and widening the circle might very well lead directly to the commitment to global perspectives many hope to see reflected in our new general education curriculum.

A second key point of reference in our past that is still real for us today is our heritage as a church-related college. The founding of Elmhurst College was certainly not distinctive in this regard. Indeed, until the arrival of the land grant universities, most colleges, especially in the Midwest, were created by churches. In

Elmhurst's case, the denominational affiliation embodies its own ever-widening circle. The roots of the German immigrant community that created Elmhurst grew out of the bitter struggles between the Lutheran and Reformed branches of European Protestantism in the seventeenth and eighteenth centuries. What was called the Evangelical Church of the Prussian Union was formed with the hope of bridging the divide between these contentious groups, and from the beginning it tried to bring an irenic—that is, peacemaking—approach to religious differences.

Immigrants from this tradition founded Eden Seminary in Missouri and then the Proseminar, or pre-seminary, at Elmhurst as a feeder. By comparison with other religious groups at the time, these German pietists put much more emphasis on doing good in the world than on fighting over doctrine. Over the years, the denomination moved in ever-widening circles just as the College did. First came the merger with the Reformed Church in the United States that created the Evangelical and Reformed or "E and R" Church, a reconciling merger strongly influenced by our own Niebuhr brothers. Then in the 1950s came the merger with the Congregational Christian Church with its New England legacy of commitment to education as well as the struggle against slavery.

The present-day United Church of Christ that resulted from this complex widening circle stands clearly on the progressive side of American Christianity with its commitments to freedom of conscience and intellect, to inclusiveness, and to the pursuit of social justice. Within this framework, Elmhurst has crafted an approach that does not wear its religiosity on its sleeve, but tries to make clear its support for the spiritual growth of all members of its religiously diverse college community. This is not a college that expects all its students to bring with them a particular set of answers, but it does invite all sorts of students to bring the full range of their questions. The irenic heritage of our founders is still recognizable in our welcome and support for students from across the wide spectrum of different traditions or no faith tradition at all.

Nowhere is the ever-widening circle more obviously demonstrated than in the long transition from an institution for young men being groomed for the pastorate in a single small denomination to a place where Catholics, Muslims, conservative Christians, Jews, secularists, agnostics, and mainline Protestants not just co-exist but interact and learn from each other. But looking back toward the center of this circle, there is no question it started with a fundamental commitment to the wholeness of the human experience, to taking seriously the questions of ultimate meaning, and to being a force for reconciliation in the world.

What might this distinctive heritage say to our college as it looks toward the future? The UCC is not at all authoritarian or prescriptive in its relationships to colleges that claim active affiliation. So what Elmhurst chooses to do with its church relationship in the future is largely up to Elmhurst. But a college founded by devout peacemakers and linked to a tradition that values inclusive communities and social justice might well have a distinctive perspective on helping to prepare its graduates for a world of deep divisions and profound ethical dilemmas. To what wider circles of useful service and faithful living might we want to introduce our students as our college moves toward broader horizons?

We come finally to a third landmark from our past that might on the surface seem the most in conflict with the principle of the ever-widening circle. Elmhurst began as a small school—a very small school, in fact. When classes first began, there were twenty-four students, and the Reverend Kranz taught all the courses while taking care of everything else as well—probably not the ideal faculty-student ratio. From then on, enrollment was a roller-coaster ride, though by any comparative standards a rather unexciting roller-coaster. Throughout the history of the College, one reads of celebratory announcements when enrollment milestones were reached. But I have yet to read about or hear from alumni of any point at which members of the College community expressed any interest at all in moving away from relatively small classes and close interaction between students and faculty and among students.

On the contrary, the thread of intimacy runs through the story of the College, and over and over, growth in numbers or facilities is interpreted as enabling the institution to be a better small college. There is an important message here for discussions of year-to-year growth and long-term optimal size. While the simple numbers are deceptively easy to read, the deeper questions have to do with the actual daily experience of students. At any given time, there are a few particular ceilings that at least appear to be absolute—the number of beds on campus, perhaps the number of parking spaces. But retracing the ever-widening circle of overall size back through the stages of the College's experience makes clear that the essence at the core is not some ideal number but the educational value of sustained, close human interaction.

What might this commitment to intimacy mean for the larger circles of the future? How might arguments about the size of the College be reframed by focusing instead on how to protect and enrich that sense of intimacy? How might this essence of the small college experience serve the differing constituencies we might invite into the Elmhurst experience? And how might emerging technology be strategically employed to maximize rather than compromise the sort of human contact that is at the core of the small college experience?

So here we have three elements of the Elmhurst saga that have been starting points for the ever-widening circles that have shaped our college—our beginnings as an international experiment, our roots in a unique faith tradition, and our heritage as a small college. In each case, the intervening years have modified and reframed but not obscured an essential quality that may help orient our thinking about the future. As we enter new stages of the continuing transition to even wider circles, we are not starting with a blank slate. This is a college with deep roots and a rich heritage. On this particular Founders Day, we are keenly aware that we are beginning to draft the next chapter in our history. Looking back helps us understand who and where we are; but it is the prospect of the journey ahead that draws us toward the possibility of even larger circles of excellence and meaning in the years to come.

No journey of great adventure is easy. There will never be enough resources, each judgment is made in the context of uncertainty, and it's plain hard work. One of the challenges for the ancient Polynesian wayfinder was that he could rarely sleep, because he could not afford to have big gaps in his memory of the journey. It is said that you could always tell which sailor was the wayfinder; he was the one with bloodshot eyes. It is so tempting to slow down, concede the power of the sea, pull in our oars, and rest. But those wider circles are still out there.

In our own faith tradition, there is a message for moments when we are on the cusp of opportunity but held back by assumptions of scarcity. Late in the book of Isaiah, the prophet likens the people of Israel to barren women who know they cannot contribute to the future. With no more children and the tents in which they live becoming empty, their lives are destined to spiral down in smaller and smaller circles. No, the prophet tells them; the future is a time when there will be so many children they should be rethinking their assumptions. Here is his startling message:

> Enlarge the place of your tent,
>
> and let the curtains of your habitation be stretched out;
>
> hold not back, lengthen your cords
>
> and strengthen your stakes.
>
> (Isaiah 54:2)

For anyone who has ever pitched a tent, the imagery is compelling. I especially like the call to pay attention to the cords and stakes. It is a useful reminder of the complexity of larger tents and the many different efforts that will contribute to the wider circles of Elmhurst's future, as the curriculum matures, as scholarship shines, as pedagogy advances, as diversity enhances, as facilities improve, as resources grow, as unanticipated hurdles are overcome, as intellectual life is energized, as new opportunities beckon, and as excellence blossoms everywhere.

Isaiah's message is one to hold close as we steer through new times of transition. Exactly how the circles of Elmhurst College will continue to widen in the coming years is not perfectly clear, nor could or should it be. But as the College takes its bearings anew and imagines a future of exciting possibilities, it is not too soon to commit ourselves to "hold not back." As one who has been deeply privileged to have had a small part in the long saga of this College, I will, over the coming years, watch with great interest and high hopes as you "enlarge the place of your tent,… lengthen your cords and strengthen your stakes."

Notes

The Doors of Learning

For more on the Royal Portal at the Cathedral of Chartres, see Jean Favier, *The World of Chartres*, Harry Abrams, Inc., 1990, and Whitney S. Stoddard, *Sculptors of the West Portals of Chartres Cathedral*, W.W. Norton & Company, 1987.

Becoming Newcomers

For a history of the first 125 years of Elmhurst College, see Melitta J. Cutright, *An Ever-Widening Circle: The Elmhurst Years*, Elmhurst College Press, 1995.

We

New York Times, August 15, 2003, p. A20.

Jared Diamond, *The Third Chimpanzee: The Evolution and Future of the Human Animal*, HarperCollins, 1992, pp. 156–157.

The Keys to the Library

William DeWitt Hyde, "Offer of the College," forward to *The College*

Man and the College Woman, Bowdoin College, 1906. Hyde was president of Bowdoin College from 1885 to 1917.

Dancing Along the Dingy Days

Emily Dickinson, "A Book," Series One, Poem 1589.

Only Connect

E. M. Forster, *Howards End*, G. P. Putnam's Sons, 1910.

Setting the Table

Ernest Hemmingway, *A Moveable Feast*, Scribner, 1964.

Emily Dickinson, "Who goes to dine must take his Feast," Series Two, Poem 1223.

"Be known to us in breaking bread," James Montgomery, *Christian Psalmist*, 1825.

Let It Shine

The story of Hamilton Naki is complicated. Obituaries appeared in *The New York Times*, *The Economist* and other newspapers on June 9–12, 2005, based on an AP report. This report stressed an account of Naki's role in the actual procedure of the first transplant, where he was said to have led the team who removed the heart from the donor. That version of the story had been widely reported, especially in the African press. On July 14, *The Economist* published a correction, citing doctors at Groote Schuur Hospital who had assured them than Naki was not involved in any way in the procedure. It would be unfortunate if the confusion over this part of Naki's saga were to overshadow his remarkable accomplishments. As *The Economist* concluded, "It is sad that the shadow of apartheid is still so long in South Africa that blacks and whites can tell the same narrative in quite different ways, each suspecting the motives of the other. And it is especially tragic that it should have involved Mr. Naki, a man considered 'wonderful' by both sides, black and white, and whose life should still be seen as an inspiration."

Strengthening the Foundations

The story of William Walker is described briefly in materials published by Winchester Cathedral, including a 1979 brochure by Canon Frederick Bussby. For a book-length treatment, see Ian T. Henderson and John Crook, *The Winchester Diver: The Saving of a Great Cathedral*, Henderson and Stirk Publishers, 1984.

Mentor's College

The quotation from *The Odyssey* is from the translation by Robert Fagles (Penguin Books, 1996).

Etched in Stone

The German inscription on Old Main reads: "*PRO-SEMINAR DER DEUTSCHEN EV. SYNODE VON N.A.*"

The Goebel Hall inscription is from John Milton, *Samson Agonistes*, lines 53–54.

The form of the Serenity Prayer selected for the Elmhurst monument, slightly altered from the 1943 original, was published by Reinhold Nie-buhr in "To Be Abased and to Abound," *The Messenger*, February 13, 1951, p. 7.

The H. Richard Niebuhr quotation is from *The Elms*, 1925, p. 16. In the original text, Niebuhr referred to the "urgent need" of "the present genera-tion of men," since this was before Elmhurst became coed.

The fountain inscription is from T. S. Eliot, *The Family Reunion*, Harcourt, Brace and Company, 1939, p. 31.

A Culture in the Wilderness

The description of Harvard's founding is by an unknown author, quoted in Richard Hofstadter and Wilson Smith, *American Higher Education: A Documentary History*, The University of Chicago Press, 1961, Vol. 1, p. 212.

The Big Promise of the Small College

Webster's argument in *The Trustees of Dartmouth College v. Woodward* is quoted in Richard Hofstadter and Wilson Smith, eds., *American Higher Education: A Documentary History*, The University of Chicago Press, 1961, Vol. 1, pp. 202–213.

Critique of a College, Swarthmore College, 1967.

Bartlett Giamatti, *A Free and Ordered Space: The Real World of the University*, W. W. Norton and Company, 1976.

Parker J. Palmer, *The Courage to Teach: Exploring the Inner Landscape of a Teacher's Life*, Jossey-Bass Publishers, 1998.

Making Music Together

Arnold Steinhardt, *Indivisible by Four: A String Quartet in Pursuit of Harmony*, Farrar, Straus and Giroux, 1998.

Old Compass, New Ocean

Paul Harris, *Peregrinations*, Vol. III.

David C. Forward, *A Century of Service: The Story of Rotary International*, Rotary International, 2003.

Kent L. Keith, *Anyway: The Paradoxical Commandments: Finding Personal Meaning in a Crazy World*, G. P. Putnam's Sons, 2001.

The Art of Associating

James T. Schleifer, *The Making of Tocqueville's Democracy in America*, The University of North Carolina Press, 1980.

Alexis de Tocqueville, *Democracy in America*, translated by Arthur Goldhammer, The Library of America, 2004.

Robert D. Putnam, *Bowling Alone: The Collapse and Revival of American Community*, Simon and Schuster, 2000.

Stephen L. Carter, *Civility: Manners, Morals, and the Etiquette of Democracy*, Basic Books, 1998.

Seeking Simplicity

The Whitehead quotation is from, *The Concept of Nature,* Cambridge University Press, 1920, p. 163.

What the Silence Is For

Randy Howe, *The Quotable Teacher*, The Lyons Press, 2003.

Max Picard, *The World of Silence*, trans. by Stanley Goodman, Regnery Gateway. Inc., 1988.

H. Richard Niebuhr, "In Quietness and in Confidence," unpublished manuscript, property of the archives of Harvard Divinity School.

Thomas Merton, "Notes for a Philosophy of Solitude," *Disputed Questions*, Farrar, Straus and Cudahy, 1960.

Ric Masten, "Robert and Nancy," from CD *Let It Be a Dance*, Sunlink Publications, 1978.

"Two people together but alone, …", Louise Lague, quoted in Dale Salwak, ed., *The Wonders of Solitude*, New World Library, 1998.

Jessica Powers, "The Christmas Silence," in Anne Fremantle, *Christmas is Here: A Catholic Selection of Stories and Poems*, Stephen Daye Press, 1955).

Let's Talk

Anatol Rapoport, *Fights, Games, and Debates*, University of Michigan, 1960.

Solvitur Ambulando

Lewis Carroll, "What the Tortoise Said to Achilles," *Mind*, n.s., 4 (1895).

Rabbi Heschel's comment is from Suzannah Heschel, "Praying With Their Feet: Remembering Abraham Joshua Heschel and Martin Luther King," *Peacework*, Issue 371, December 2006–January 2007.

St. Augustine, Sermon 169.

Here There Be Dragons

Euripides, *Helen*, translated by Richard Lattimore.

David Gross, quoted in *The New York Times*, October 19, 2004, p. D3.

Rudyard Kipling, "The English Flag."

Gwendolyn Brooks, "Paul Robeson."

Who's in Charge Here?

Victor Frankl, *Man's Search for Meaning*, Beacon Press, 1959.

The Memory Holes of the Wampanoag

George Orwell, *1984*, Harcourt Brace and Company, 1949.

Edward Winslow, *Good Newes from New England: a true Relation of things very remarkable at the Plantation of Plimoth in New England*, Applewood Books, (originally published in 1624).

Nathaniel Philbrick, *Mayflower: A Story of Courage, Community, and War*, Viking, 2006.

Wider Circles for Elmhurst College

For more on Polynesian wayfinders, see David Lewis, *We, the Navigators: The Ancient Art of Landfinding in the Pacific*, University of Hawaii Press, 1994.